ESSAYS ON BIBLICAL PREACHING

Titles in the Jay Adams Library

The Christian Counselor's Casebook
The Christian Counselor's Manual
Competent to Counsel
Essays on Biblical Preaching
Essays on Counseling
Handbook of Church Discipline
How to Help People Change
Insight and Creativity in Christian Counseling
The Language of Counseling and the Christian Counselor's Wordbook
Lectures on Counseling
Marriage, Divorce, and Remarriage in the Bible
Preaching With Purpose
Shepherding God's Flock
Solving Marriage Problems
A Theology of Christian Counseling
Update on Christian Counseling, Volumes 1 and 2

ESSAYS ON BIBLICAL PREACHING

Jay E. Adams

Zondervan Publishing House • Grand Rapids, MI

ESSAYS ON BIBLICAL PREACHING
Copyright © 1982, 1983 by Jay E. Adams

MINISTRY RESOURCES LIBRARY is an imprint of
Zondervan Publishing House, 1415 Lake Drive, S.E.,
Grand Rapids, Michigan 49506

Library of Congress Cataloging in Publication Data
Adams, Jay Edward.
    Essays on Biblical preaching.

    (The Jay Adams library)
    "Ministry resources library."
    1. Preaching. I. Adams, Jay Edward. Preaching to the heart. 1986.
II. Title. III. Series: Adams, Jay Edward. Jay Adams library.
BV4211.2.A334 1986   251   86-11047
ISBN 0-310-51041-4

All rights reserved. No part of this publication may be reproduced, stored in a retrieval system, or transmitted in any form or by any means—electronic, mechanical, photocopy, recording, or any other—except for brief quotations in printed reviews, without prior permission of the publisher.

Printed in the United States of America

86 87 88 89 90 91 92 / 10 9 8 7 6 5 4 3 2 1

CONTENTS

Truth Apparent

Preface
Introduction

1. I Heard It—Did You? ... 1
2. Good Preaching Is Hard Work ... 4
3. What Kinds of Preaching Are There? ... 7
4. Preaching with Purpose ... 9
5. More—On Purpose ... 14
6. Maintaining Balance ... 20
7. Preaching the Gospel in the Church ... 23
8. Some Neglected Subjects ... 26
9. Using the Original Languages in Preaching ... 29
10. Adaptation Through Audience Analysis ... 32
11. Preaching and Writing ... 36
12. Making Preaching a Pleasure ... 39
13. Outlining ... 47
14. Don't Tell Us What You Are Going to Do—Do It ... 53
15. Illustrating God's Truth ... 55
16. More on "Illustrations" ... 61
17. Imagine That! ... 64
18. Make Your Preaching Live ... 67
19. Preaching Rhythms ... 73
20. Does This Apply to You? ... 76
21. Preaching With Personalized How-to ... 82
22. Bodily Action in Preaching ... 87
23. A Study of Taped Sermons ... 92
24. The Young Preacher ... 97
25. A Suggestion for Young Preachers ... 99

Preaching to the Heart

1. Introduction 1
2. What Is the Heart? 3
3. Two Kinds of Hearts 7
4. Preaching From the Heart 11
5. Boldness of Heart 15
6. Preaching From God's Heart 22
7. Heart-Convicting Preaching 26
8. A Heart-Adapted Form 31
9. Conclusion 34

Truth Apparent

To
those faithful servants
of the Word
who care enough to
make
God's
truth apparent

PREFACE

Truth Apparent suddenly came into being. Over a period of several years I have been writing articles on preaching for *The Journal of Pastoral Practice*. Because I planned to publish a comprehensive homiletics textbook, I gathered all of these essays together to see if I could use them as the basis for several chapters in that larger work. But on reading them through I quickly came to the conclusion that there was no good way to do this. Their form was so different from the form I had in mind for the textbook that they would all have to be extensively revised. The effort, I concluded, would cost more time and energy than it was worth—and I was not sure that, in the end, I would have anything even remotely approximating what I desired. So, I decided to lay them aside and begin writing the homiletics text from the foundation up.

Yet, as I read over them I was sure that there was much material that would be useful to many persons as it stands, or with a minimum amount of revision. Moreover, the textbook might take much longer to write than I had originally imagined, since I had now determined to develop it independently from scratch. "These essays were designed to stand on their own," I concluded; "so why not let them? After all," I reasoned, "more people should read a book of essays on preaching than will read them in a string of journals." So, with careful revision, I prepared them for the present volume.

But there were some other items that were needed in order to round out the book with emphases other than those found in the articles from the *Journal*. I added new articles written in much the same style.

It is my prayer that in this way I shall be able to help many preachers, seminary students, and other Christian speakers improve the quality of their preaching and speaking even sooner than I had expected. And, at the same time, I trust that a separate homiletic textbook will be able to meet the needs of seminaries and other training institutions in a more systematic way.

The materials in this book roam over the entire corpus of the field of homiletics. They should be found useful for individual study and, in more formal contexts, as supplementary reading to accompany classroom lectures. They would be especially useful as required reading for a practice-preaching course in which something brief, pointed, and provocative is required.

May the Spirit Himself, if He so pleases, determine how best this book may be used to help ministers of the Word to be more faithful and effective in the proclamation of His inerrant truth.

Jay E. Adams
The Millhouse, 1982

Instead, we have renounced shameful, hidden activities, refusing to walk in craftiness or to adulterate God's Word. But by making the truth apparent, we commend ourselves to every person's conscience in God's sight (II Cor. 4:2).

INTRODUCTION

Preaching has not deteriorated all that much; that is not why there is so much "poor preaching" around today. What has happened is that congregational standards have been raised. Preaching is now judged over against the other forms of speaking heard every day on TV and radio, and against such standards the communication heard on Sundays often falls far short. The truth of the matter seems to be that preachers simply can't get away with it any more!

There was a time the preacher was called the *parson, the* "person" in town—the most prominent, well-respected and, usually, the *best educated* person around. He was respected for his learning and language as well as for his work's sake; apart from a few doctors and lawyers, he was likely to be the only person with a graduate education and, indeed, in many places the only one with any college education at all. In those early days, there was no TV to compete with; the only other speaking that was heard was done by an occasional trial lawyer or a politician. The "parson" was *the* speaker in town.

That is no longer the case. Good speaking—grammatically correct, articulate, and interesting—flows from skilled professionals through the various audio media; a flip of the switch and it is yours. It has become commonplace. Moreover, many adults themselves are college trained, some of whom also hold graduate degrees. They themselves are used to speaking good English, as well as hearing it. And on Sunday, when they go to church, they expect to encounter speaking that is at least as good as what they produce and consume all week long.

Is it too much to ask preachers to conform to speaking standards that measure up to newscasters? Should the daily news be presented more persuasively and grippingly than the Good News? Surely not. Well, then, something must be done. And you must do it. It is your task as a minister of the Word, a seminary student, or a Christian worker to pay attention to this matter. You must do *more* than your fathers; you must speak *better* than your peers. While it will never again be true that you will be the only speaker in town, it could be (and should be) true that you are the *best* speaker around. You start with a great advantage—you have the best message of all, you have a congregation that has gathered to hear it. Is it expecting too much then, under those conditions, to produce good, very good, preaching of the Word of the living God, preaching that commands attention and respect even from today's linguistically sophisticated masses? Certainly not. But, in order to acquire such preaching ability you must be willing to spend time working on your speaking practices. To peruse the older volumes on preaching will not do; the standards set forth in them differ considerably from the ones required of you today. For their day they may have been acceptable; for ours they are not. An emphasis on the man himself and on content permeates these works; there is far less emphasis on form. While in no way neglecting these two essential ingredients of effective preaching, today there must be also a new focus on form. And the form that is followed in many respects will differ from the form that was advocated a generation ago. That form was a modified holdover from the standards and practices of medieval times, a form that has been abandoned by other sectors of society and must be abandoned by the ministry as well.

That new form, and how to make a transition to it, is what this book is all about. Today it is our task, no less than it was Paul's, to communicate with those who need to hear the truth. And, with Paul, we too must abandon gimmicks and clever means of preaching. With him, we should be concerned about "making the truth apparent." Unless and until it is presented in ways that will be heard by twentieth-century man, we will continue to fail in our mission. It is my hope, therefore, that you will take seriously the ideas presented in *Truth Apparent* and will see fit to incorporate many of its numerous suggestions in an attempt to become a more effective communicator of the gospel.

The concern expressed in this book is not to turn out orators, the fame of whose rhetorical prowess will be spoken far and wide; no, rather it is (1) to help you get out of the way of the message so that the listener hears and concentrates on what God says rather than on the foibles of the one communicating His message, and (2) to help you develop a preaching method that will enable you to discover and deliver that message in the purest and most unadulterated manner possible.

1
I HEARD IT—DID YOU?

A rare thing happened the other day—I heard a good sermon. Let me briefly analyze it for you, noting some of the factors that made it good.

First, it was *preaching;* it was not a string of stories or a stodgy lecture. By that I mean, from start to finish, the sermon was directed to *us*. We were involved from the outset. The truth of the passage was presented as God's message to *us*, not only to the members of a church long ago and far away in biblical times. God became significant to us as Someone living, ruling, caring *now*—for *us*. The preacher made us concerned, and kept us concerned, about *our* church, *our* community.

Next, what I heard was *biblical* preaching. What he preached was not an essay on some truth, not the ideas of politicians, media personalities, philosophers, theologians or his own opinion, but what *God* said to us in Paul's letter. Not only did he tell us what the preaching portion means, but he even showed us just how every point that he made comes from the biblical passage. Because he did so, we were able to evaluate for ourselves whether the preacher's conclusions about the text were accurate. Significantly, it was apparent that he had done his homework and that what he told us made sense. And, I believe others in the congregation, if asked, would agree with me that what he said about the text was accurate. He satisfied us that he was preaching what Paul had said. We went away understanding the passage and how everything in the sermon flowed from it. Consequently, we listened to his exhortations about our lives, not as the opinions of a man, but as a word from God to us. He preached, and his preaching was received, with an authority appropriate to the sort of message that it was. We left knowing that we had heard a proclamation from God.

Again, the sermon was *interesting*. The preacher did not cook the juice out of the passage, leaving hard, dry, burned-over, abstract teaching. Nor did he serve it to us as a raw, bloody, uncooked chunk of meat. Like a fine chef, he knew just how to handle the passage, cooking it to a turn, garnishing and accenting it so that what he served was the text in full flavor. Its own nutritious juices were preserved, and where delicate nuances otherwise might be missed, he seasoned it with illustrations that brought them out. As he delivered it, the sermon sizzled!

Moreover, the sermon was well *organized*. There were points, sturdy as steel, undergirding the whole, arranged in logical order. But the points did not protrude; he did not bore us with unnecessary firstlies, secondlies, and thirdlies; he avoided details that added nothing to the central idea of the message, and—believe it or not—he did not bother us with distracting, forced alliteration. His entire focus in the sermon was on the intent of the Holy Spirit in the text. He kept moving ahead, avoiding all meaningless prefacing and repetition, instead skillfully thrusting each point straight into our hearts! And the sermon was evangelical; he preached the gospel—clearly—but it was not merely another evangelistic sermon. There was meat for believers. Yet that meat had been marinated in the truth of the cross.

Now, I know that you will find it difficult to believe me when I tell you that, on top of everything else, that sermon was *practical*. Yes, it really was! It was carefully adapted to the particular congregation to which it was preached. And the preacher persisted in telling us not only *what* to do but *how* to do it. And sometimes, like his Lord in the Sermon on the Mount, he also told us how not to do it. It was plain that he had spent time thinking about what biblical principles mean in everyday living and had worked out biblically derived applications and implementations of each one.

What a sermon it was! You don't hear many like it today. Indeed, because of this fact, you may wonder where it was preached and who preached it. You may ask, "Are cassette tapes available?" The answer is no. But I can tell you where I heard it—it was in a reverie while sitting in the Montreal airport that I heard that sermon, and the only record of it is the one that I am now sketching for you enroute to Moncton. But, is it doomed to remain merely a bare record, hidden away from the people of God in a pastoral journal sitting on your shelf? Why should it? Why don't you bring it to life? Why don't you preach it this Sunday to *your* congregation? Then if you, and scores of other preachers with you, do so, thousands of people throughout the land will truly be able to say, "I heard a good sermon today!"

2
GOOD PREACHING IS HARD WORK

I have had the opportunity to hear much preaching over the last few years, some very good, some mediocre, most very bad. What is the problem with preaching? There is no *one* problem, of course; there are a number of problems to which I have been addressing myself over the years. But if there is one thing that stands out, it is the problem I mention today.

What I am about to say may not strike you as being as specific as other things I have written, yet I believe it is at the bottom of a number of other difficulties. My point is that good preaching demands hard work. From listening to sermons and from talking to hundreds of preachers about preaching, I am convinced that the basic reason for poor preaching is the failure to spend adequate time and energy in preparation. Many preachers—perhaps most—simply don't work long enough on their sermons.

You may question my charge, and (of course) you may be one of the notable exceptions to what, regrettably, has become the rule. Good! But if so, remember, you are an exception. For the rest of you, note well, I did not say that preachers don't work hard; for the most part I believe that Bible-believing preachers work *very* hard—probably too hard! And, indeed, therein may lie the clue to the problem: many work so hard *at everything else* that, as a result, they neglect their preparation for the ministry of the Word.

Not enough time is spent either in doing the historical-grammatical-*telic* (purpose-oriented) exegesis of the preaching portion or in thinking through the format, form, and style in which the message ought to be presented to the particular congregation to which it will be delivered. Inadequate study of the biblical text means that the purpose of the preaching portion will not be clear to the preacher himself. When that is true, there is no way in which he can make it clear to his hearers.

But even when adequate time has been given for the preacher to discover the *telos* (i.e., the Holy Spirit's purpose) in the preaching portion, there is still the matter of allotting the time necessary to produce the best outline, to work out the most appropriate language, to develop the right sort of illustrations, and to think through concrete recommendations for implementation. And, care must be taken to adapt all of this work to the peculiar knowledge, circumstances, background, etc., of the particular body of people to whom the message will be delivered. That too takes time and study; there is no easier way to arrive at a good congregational analysis.

From what I see and hear, *very* little time is devoted to such work. Yet, without work on form, the best exegesis falls flat on the floor.

"But," you protest, "I have so little time. I'd like to do more of what you say, but I simply don't see any place in my schedule for it."

Granted, you may not have room in your schedule for it, but that just proves my point—you are working *hard, too hard*, at the wrong things. You must *make* room. Preaching is a high priority item; others of a lesser priority must go.

Let me ask you some pointed questions. An honest answer to these will help you to re-evaluate your priorities. But before you answer, remember how much the apostles had to do and how the Bible teaches that they handled this very problem:

> So the Twelve called a general meeting of the disciples and said, "It isn't right for us to stop preaching God's Word to serve tables. Now then, brothers, look for seven of your men who have a good reputation, full of the Spirit and wisdom, that we may appoint them to this work, while we continue to devote ourselves to prayer and the ministry of the Word" (Acts 6:2-4).

1. Do you pray earnestly for the members of your congregation?
2. Do you waste time on the telephone, talking about matters that others could handle?
3. How much TV do you watch each week?
4. How much time do you spend in committee meetings?
5. What are you doing that someone else in the congregation could do instead of you?

I could ask any number of other questions like these, but I don't think it is necessary to do so. We can all find the time to do whatever God wants us to do—if we only search for it.

One reason why pastors lose so much time is because they have not disciplined themselves to say "no." The way to say "no" with freedom is to have a carefully planned schedule that does not permit you to say "yes" to events that you ought to avoid. Nothing frees one up so much as a well-planned schedule. Such a schedule is planned in terms of God's *priorities*.

In Acts 6:2, the apostles allotted time in terms of priorities when they set the ministry of the Word (preaching and counseling) above waiting on tables. That was not snobbery; it was dedication to divine duty. Today, as in their time, whether he knows it or not, whenever a pastor says, "I don't have the time," he is really saying, "I am misusing my time waiting on tables." Discover which tables you currently are serving, delegate them to your deacons, and start giving that time to prayer and the ministry of the Word—especially to preaching!

3

WHAT KINDS OF PREACHING ARE THERE?

For a long while we have been told that there are three kinds of preaching: expository, topical (or doctrinal), and textual. Other than as indicators of emphasis, these distinctions are sheer nonsense and have served mainly to create confusion and have done more harm than good.

In all good preaching the three are never really separated; it is in poor preaching alone that you find this separation taking place. For instance, poor "expository preachers" think of exposition as merely making a running commentary on a passage of Scripture for a given length of time, covering any number of areas, with applications interspersed, and coming to an end only when the clock runs out. Poor "topical preachers" take a topic or theme, totally apart from Scripture (or using some Scripture as a springboard), and spout off pious platitudes and truths with no regard to exposition at all. They act as if congregations were to believe them because *they* said it. Poor "textual preachers" take a verse or two, a portion of a verse, or a word, and expatiate on that totally (or almost totally) out of context. All of these *poor* approaches to preaching have been occasioned by this foolish and artificial division between what is called textual, topical, and expository preaching.

The truth is that in every good sermon all three are present. There must always be a text, or (as I have called it) a "preaching portion." This is the passage (or passages) that form the God-given basis for all that the preacher says. The text may be long or short, according to the length of material necessary to present a *telic* or purpose portion (see "Preaching with Purpose" elsewhere in this book). There will be a topic. How could one preach if he has no subject (or topic) to preach about? If he confines himself to a *telic* unit of material as his preaching portion, however, his exposition will not run across many varied topics; there will be *one* only. The topical (doctrinal) emphasis may include the use of more than one passage of Scripture, but the use of these passages (probably two, and no more than three or four) requires even more incisive exposition (of each passage, with its *telic* emphasis and these *tele* brought into careful relationship to one another and the doctrine). Good preaching, then, while emphasizing one of the three aspects of preaching, will always include all three. There will a text (a *telic* unit as a preaching portion), a topic (whatever is the subject, or teaching, of the preaching portion), and exposition (the work of the preacher to demonstrate that the purpose he teaches is actually the Holy Spirit's purpose in the text, and that is the sole authority for what he says). If your preaching doesn't include all three, as well as application and implementation of truth, there is something lacking.

4

PREACHING WITH PURPOSE

For years now I have told my students that on Sunday morning if I were to awaken them at 3 o'clock and ask, "What is the general purpose of your sermon today?" and at 3:15 a.m. I were to ask, "What is your specific purpose?" they ought to know the answers so well that they could spit them out in a crisp, one-sentence response ("My general purpose is to inform"; "My specific purpose is to inform the congregation about the facts of death and resurrection listed in I Thessalonians 4") and roll over and go back to sleep.

"You're kidding!" you say. "Is purpose all that important?" You'd better believe it. Unless a preacher knows the purpose of his sermon, all is lost. He himself is lost, the congregation will soon get lost, and the sermon would be better if it were lost. "Well, if purpose is so important, why didn't they teach me about it in my seminary homiletics courses?"

Let me answer that question by telling you a fact. The truth is that I have actually done what I am about to suggest to you. Stand in the homiletic section of the stacks of the library of any large theological seminary, and with eyes closed reach at random for several volumes of sermons. Then open these volumes, again at random, and study the sermons on those pages. You will discover two things:
1. No discernible purpose will be present in half or more of them.
2. Where there is a purpose, it will be the preacher's own purpose rather than the purpose of the biblical writer whose words are "used" for a purpose different from the one that he has in mind.

The importance of discerning and preaching according to the Holy Spirit's purpose has not been emphasized in exegesis or in homiletics courses. Yet, *nothing* is more fundamental to solid biblical preaching.

Consider these facts: if you don't discover the Holy Spirit's purpose

in each preaching portion and make it your purpose too, in preaching from that passage you will
1. distort the meaning of the Scriptures,
2. lose the authority of the Scriptures in preaching, and
3. confuse congregations while failing to feed them.

Suppose I were to write you a letter of application for a position as the assistant pastor of your church. And suppose, upon receipt of this letter, you were to begin investigating all the facts you could about me and the letter itself in order to understand exactly what it said. You studied the time and place of writing. You did a background study on my life and activities. You compared vocabulary, word usage, and the basic theology of this letter with other materials written by me. Finally, after some time doing such things, you concluded that you understood precisely what the letter was all about—and stopped with that! Why, the purpose of the letter would be frustrated, wouldn't it? I wanted you to give me a job; not merely study all the facts about me and my request. This study would be fine, if at length it led to a consideration of the purpose of the letter. But of what use is all of your work if it doesn't? Yet, much study and preaching of a passage of the Scriptures is just like that—everything else about the passage is carefully investigated and weighed, but the Holy Spirit's purpose in writing it is ignored.

When I speak of the Holy Spirit's purpose in writing a portion of the Scriptures, what I have in mind by "purpose" is *what He intends to do to the reader*. In every passage that He inspired, the Holy Spirit (unlike many preachers) had some intention, some purpose, in view. It is the preacher's task to discover not only what He intended to do to the reader, but also to make that same purpose his own in preaching to the listener. The preacher has no right to use a portion of the Scriptures for his own purposes; he must discover the Spirit's purpose in a passage and preach from that passage to achieve that purpose and that purpose alone. When preachers begin to take this matter seriously there will be more power in their preaching (the Spirit blesses *His* Word) and more understanding of the Scriptures by the congregation. There will be less heresy, fewer scripturally detached essays, and less wasted effort and time.

"But," you insist, "why hasn't someone told me about purpose before this?" Well, remember the books in the stacks? It has been the preachers who have taught the preachers to teach the preachers over the years. And false views of preaching have prevailed as the same errors have been perpetuated from generation to generation. You can't expect men who have been guilty of the practice of using the Scriptures for their own purposes to teach others to do otherwise, can you?

But it is time for this general practice, with all of its attendant evils, to be brought to an end. One thing and one thing alone can do so—a focus on purpose as the controlling factor in the study, construction, and delivery of every sermon.

Purpose is not only the controlling factor in selecting and studying a passage of Scripture for preaching,[1] it is the unifying factor in all that is done. Anything that doesn't contribute to the furthering of the Holy Spirit's purpose should be eliminated from the sermon; everything that does should be retained. Purpose determines the kind of outline. If the purpose is informative, the outline should protrude; if it is motivational, it should recede. Purpose influences language too. Informative material calls for one sort of language, motivational language calls for another. So, it is clear, purpose is *the* controlling factor in preaching. No wonder all is lost without a clear purpose.

There are two kinds of purpose (as my earlier comments indicated): general and specific. Every sermon, just as every preaching portion, has a general purpose and a specific purpose. But what is a "preaching portion"? It is any unit of scriptural material (a sentence, a paragraph, or a chapter) that has both a general purpose and a specific purpose. If you isolate a portion from which to preach that doesn't have these purposes, it will be inadequate; it is not a preaching portion. "Jesus wept," though many sermons have been preached on it, is not a preaching portion for this reason. Purpose, then, is the first factor in selecting a portion from which to preach. These may be larger portions with larger purposes (of course) or smaller ones that are actually portions containing sub-purposes or even sub-sub-purposes. The Bible has purpose (cf. II Tim. 3:15-17); each book of the Bible has purpose (cf. John 20:30, 31); each section of each book has purpose too (cf. I Thess. 4:13-18).

---

1. What I shall call the "preaching portion."

General purposes in the Bible can be reduced to three: to inform, to persuade, to motivate. Any one of these three will seldom appear alone, but usually there will be an *emphasis* on one or the other. When Paul says, "I would not have you to be ignorant, brethren, concerning . . . ," his general purpose is informative. But upon concluding his remarks, he says, "So, comfort one another with these words" (a motivational purpose). Incidentally, the Bible abounds with these purpose cues ("These things are written that . . . ," "I write to stir up your . . . ," etc.). Look for them. But purposes also occur without such cues.

Specific purposes are the particular objects of general ones. When Paul writes, "I would not have you to be ignorant, brethren, concerning . . . ," it is that "concerning" which he would not have them to remain ignorant about that constitutes his specific purpose. So, a motivational purpose means to have as one's purpose to motivate one to _____. Whatever one fills in the blank is the specific purpose. A persuasive purpose could be stated this way: "I want to persuade my congregation to believe (disbelieve) _____." Again, fill in the blank with the specific purpose.

Without purpose, one simply preaches, but with no aim in view. The old saying that "If one aims at nothing he is sure to hit it," surely holds true of preaching. Let me encourage you, therefore, to write out at the top of every sermon (not a proposition, not a thematic statement, not a central idea, but) a *purpose* statement. Its form may look something like this:

$$\text{I want to} \begin{Bmatrix} \text{inform} \\ \text{persuade} \\ \text{motivate} \end{Bmatrix} \text{my congregation to} \begin{Bmatrix} \text{learn about} \\ \text{believe, disbelieve} \\ \text{do} \end{Bmatrix}$$

_____ (fill in the specific purpose).

I believe that what I have said about purpose is the most important word I could speak to you about preaching. If you take it to heart, it could be a vital factor in your ministry.

Start working on this matter today. It will take some time to develop fully your ability to discover purpose and preach with purpose, but unless you begin working at it prayerfully and carefully, it will never happen on its own. Instead, you must determine to preach with purpose, on purpose, of course.

5
MORE—ON PURPOSE

I have assigned purpose the crucial place in preaching. I should now like to add a word or two to what I have said already.

The Preaching Portion

Purpose becomes the basic means for determining a preaching portion. There are many types of literature in the Bible—narrative, poetry, proverb, parable, letters, apocalyptic, to name some of the principal literary types. The proverb can be one sentence long, the narrative several pages. How then does a preacher determine the size of the portion from which he will preach a given sermon? The answer is simple, and it avoids the arbitrary way in which so many ministers make the choice: a section of Scripture becomes a preaching portion when—and only when—it is a purpose unit. That is to say you don't arbitrarily select a portion of a certain length as your preaching portion because (presumably) it appears to have enough (and not too much) material in it. Blackwood used to tell us in class, "The paragraph ordinarily will be your text." But the arbitrary nature of this rule (which in a rough way often works) is apparent when preaching through Proverbs (especially from chapter 10 on) or (on the other hand) when preaching from a parable two or three paragraphs long or from a historical narrative in I or II Kings. There, you see, the rule falls apart. Better is the rule that I am suggesting—always choose *a unit of material* that the Holy Spirit has *given to achieve a particular purpose*.

The unit may be large with a correspondingly large purpose (containing sub-purposes). But what holds it together as a unit is the fact that it was intended to achieve one particular overall purpose. There may be smaller sub-purposes (all of which contribute to the larger, umbrella purpose), but when preaching from this larger unit, the smaller purpose units must serve the larger one throughout the sermon. Such a larger purpose unit may consist of an entire book like III John or Jude.

The danger here is to get sidetracked into preaching on one or more of the sub-purposes in the book (e.g., III John, vv. 6-8 may turn the sermon largely into a missionary message, whereas the overall thrust of this stopgap letter is to let Gaius know that he, not Diotrephes, has done the right thing, and that he should continue to do so). If you find your sermon becoming unbalanced, over-weighted toward one or more sub-units, then that is the sign that (1) you should break it up into a series of sermons, or (2) you should save the other units for later sermons, or (3) you must resist the temptation and stick to the larger overall purpose.

III John can be preached either as one sermon or as a series of eight or nine sermons (I have done both), depending upon whether you preach the overall purposes or the sub-purposes. Of course, when you do the latter, you must never forget the general purpose that the specific sub-purpose units were intended to support. That means they may not be preached *in isolation* but always *in relation to* the larger thrust.

When preaching from the book of Jude (which was intended to get believers to contend for the faith when the church was invaded by apostates and libertines), it is not proper (for example) to preach a sermon on "soul winning" from verses 22, 23. If, in a series of 11 or 12 messages, you mark off these verses (rightly) as verses containing a sub-purpose, then this sub-purpose must be understood in the light of the overall purpose and preached that way. Accordingly, verses 22, 23 would be seen as instructions to the faithful believer about how to rescue from the fires *of apostasy* others who have been (or are in danger of being) trapped in them. Each of the three types of persons (the continued occurrences of triplets in Jude settles the textual question for me) demands a different approach, as Jude points out. It is possible, of course, to develop even three sermons on these three approaches—after all, the Holy Spirit's purpose was to distinguish three such problems demanding three distinct approaches. If your congregation needs such information in detail, it might be important to take the time to develop each approach fully. Yet, in doing so, you must recognize what you have done. You have opted for preaching each of three sermons from a sub-sub-purpose. That is OK, because these are clearly purpose units (and, therefore, preaching portions). But there is always even a greater danger of preaching these in isolation than if verses 22, 23 formed your preaching portion. You must be careful, therefore, to preach these under the double umbrella of the larger purposes:

JUDE

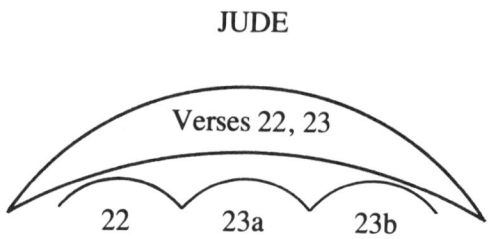

In emphasis, in the first of these three sermons, you will continue to talk about contending for the faith (overall umbrella), by rescuing from the fires of apostasy (sub-purpose umbrella of vv. 22, 23) persons who doubt (sub-sub-purpose umbrella of v. 22), etc.

The Outline

Having exhausted that question (hopefully not you), let's move to a second matter—the outline. I'll want to say much more about outlines later on, but for now just let me handle one or two issues.

What basically determines the form of the outline? The preacher? The congregation? The text? No, although all three of these elements contribute something to it, as I shall show in another place. But basically the form of the outline is determined again by the purpose of the Holy Spirit in the preaching portion.

"What? Do you mean that I am not supposed to find the outline form in the preaching portion itself?" That's exactly what I mean! And it isn't heresy to say so, either. In what New Testament sermon (Acts is full of them, and some of Paul's epistles obviously contain sermonic material[1]) do you ever hear the preacher say to his con-

---

1. Paul used an emanuensis, and he was fundamentally a preacher. Can't you see him getting wound up and preaching as he verbally writes many of his letters?

gregation, "This passage naturally falls into three points"? That isn't how you ought to preach a text, unless it is sermonic material[2] to begin with.[3]

Unless working with material already in sermonic form, what you do when you allow the textual form to determine the outline form is to let content in non-sermonic form dictate how a sermon is to be preached! That doesn't make much sense, does it? Evidently the New Testament preachers didn't think it wise to do so, because they *didn't*.

If there are narrative forms, apocalyptic and letter forms, poetic, proverbial and parabolic forms, etc., then you are going to have to learn to "translate" your material from such a form into a preaching form. After all, you aren't in the pulpit to tell stories, recite poetry, or dictate letters! You are there to preach. Neither are you there to talk about the poetic or proverbial form of the preaching portion; a sermon is not a literary analysis of the Bible! Yet much supposed "exposition" is little more than that. Your form, then, must be verbal, not literary; it must grow out of and conform to the purpose of the portion as this best can be conveyed verbally to a given congregation.

That gives you great flexibility (and larger responsibility) in developing the preaching form in such a way that it best gets across the Holy Spirit's purpose in the preaching portion. There is the same freedom for adaption to circumstances that Paul exercised when preaching to different groups with slightly differing purposes in view.[4] It is the freedom that is in evidence all through the New Testament, wherever preaching occurs or is discussed. In contrast, our arbitrary forms come not from the Bible but from Middle Age Scholasticism. Let's not try to be more pious than Paul. We must not let the traditions of men since his time limit the freedom of the Scriptures.

This freedom means that though in the preaching portion there were only two points (most Hebrew poetry and proverbial material is built by parallelism) you may want to have three, or one. Good! Go ahead, just so long as what you say grows out of the preaching portion itself.

2. Ibid.
3. Because much of Paul's material is, his letters often do.
4. Cf. my *Studies in Preaching*, vol. II, "Audience Adaptation in the Sermons and Speeches of Paul," for more detail.

"Can I rearrange the *order* of the material?" Certainly! The order in the preaching portion may appear because you are preaching from an acrostic psalm, not because of logical or persuasive reasons. The acrostic order was intended to aid memory and recall and served that purpose. Unless that also is your purpose, feel free to change it.[5]

Announcing Points?

"Well! I'm really shook up by all this! But since we're getting so radical, let me ask one more question. Do I still have to announce each point to the congregation, or may I preach now and then with smoother transitions? You know what I mean—do I have to say, 'My first point today is . . .'?" Of course you don't. Where in the Bible do you ever see this happen? Did Paul on Mars Hill say, "Now my sermon falls into three points today. My first point is . . .'"?

Let your purpose determine whether your points will be announced. For *yourself*, of course, you must have a solid outline, clearly worked out, but *don't ever announce your points unless that will help your congregation understand or more clearly remember the Holy Spirit's purpose.*

Purpose, then, again becomes the determining factor. If the general purpose of the preaching portion is to *inform,* it may be well to announce the points to your congregation (if in this way they can see that "there are two kinds—and *only* two—of people in the world: saved and lost," or if there are *"three steps* to peace that must be taken *in the following order"*). Clearly, there is good reason for announcing your points in such cases. In other words, there is a good *purpose* for doing so.

But let's say that your general purpose is to persuade to believe (or disbelieve) a truth (or error). Then there would be no special reason for announcing, "There are three reasons for believing. . . ." You are not concerned about whether the listener knows how many reasons there are for believing (unless that *is* the point); you simply want him to believe. The same is true if your purpose is to motivate: you aren't concerned about memory; what you are after is action.[6]

5. You'd probably have to do so anyway, because English and Hebrew words don't begin with the same letters.
6. See my *Pulpit Speech* for more on these three general purposes.

A good rule of thumb is this: if announcing points in a sermon isn't helpful (and it isn't unless it serves a *purpose*), then *it gets in the way*. Anything that doesn't help hurts. Everything in the sermon should contribute to furthering the purpose. If it doesn't make it clearer, more memorable, more persuasive, it hinders. Do nothing to hinder. The regular, mechanical announcement of divisions in a sermon nine times out of ten is not helpful. It is better, therefore, *not* to announce points unless you can see a good purpose for doing it in a given message.

6

MAINTAINING BALANCE

Obviously extremes are bad; God is not the God of extremes, but the God of the scriptural center. In all things there is a biblical balance—predestination may not be preached to the exclusion of human responsibility (or the reverse); faith without works is dead, works without faith in Hebrews are called "dead works," etc. It is about maintaining one such balance *in preaching* that I wish to append just this brief note. Yet the brevity of what I have to say must not make you think it unimportant. Actually, it is (perhaps) the most important point of all.

There is a tendency for conservative preachers to err in either of two directions:
1. They may preach the gospel, and hardly anything else but the gospel.
2. They may preach the rest of the counsel of God *as if it were unrelated to the gospel.*

Both extremes do a decided disservice to God and to His Word.

I am not going to elaborate on the kind of preaching that sees the way of salvation—*and nothing but* the way of salvation—in every passage. Usually, connected with it is a runaway typology, excessive story telling and . . . well, you know the rest. The "whole counsel of God" consists of far more than the way of salvation. The writer of Hebrews wanted to get on with other things as well (Heb. 6:1-3). He didn't want to linger over the milk bottle any longer; he wanted to "go on to maturity" by feeding his readers "solid food" (5:11-14; 6:1). It would be wrong to keep working on a foundation that had already been laid (6:1). So, too, must every preacher of the Word do the hard work of learning and teaching far more than the gospel message.

Those who err in not feeding, building, and perfecting the saints, once they have shed their diapers and are ready for long pants, often justify their exclusive gospel preaching by speaking about the "evangelistic outreach" of the church. But evangelism, *principally*, ought to be carried on by *all* the members of the church (Acts 8:4) largely *outside* of the regular meetings of the body. Not a single person is evangelized in a Christian worship service in the book of Acts (the New Testament manual for evangelism). The major emphasis of preaching *within the body* is on "all things" that Christ commanded. The New Testament Epistles themselves provide good evidence of that sort of preaching.

One wonders whether, at bottom, it is always zeal for evangelism that motivates a ministry of gospel-only preaching. Could it not be—in many instances—the *easy* way? Isn't it easier to find the gospel everywhere, attach a few interesting stories to the message, and then conclude with a long invitation? Too often, I am afraid, lack of preparation, poor knowledge of the true purposes of passages, and the like, is what is really behind this type of preaching.

On the other hand, there are ministries—often styled "teaching," or "expository" ministries—in which the gospel rarely (if ever) is preached, except when interpreting those passages to which one comes as he moves along in a book in which the gospel stands out so plainly that it can hardly be missed. (Even here, the discussion may be *about* the gospel rather than a proclamation of the good news itself, that "Christ died for our sins . . . and rose again on the third day." Such teaching is justified by a misuse of Ephesians 4:11, 12.

Some of the sermons that are preached from this opposite extreme are so devoid of the gospel that they could have been preached in a Jewish synagogue or in a liberal church without ruffling a feather. No sermon by a Bible-believing pastor ought ever be acceptable in either place. (I am not thinking of talks especially prepared for either audience; what I mean is that his regular messages in his own church ought to be so distinctively Christian that *none* of them could ever be mistaken for anything less than truly Christian.)

What, then, must one do? Here are two suggestions.

1. Always include a clear statement of the gospel in every message, *even* though most regularly preached messages (strictly speaking) will not be evangelistic. That is to say, all messages ought to proclaim—in one way or another—that belief in Jesus Christ as Savior is essential to understanding or doing (or

doing for the right reasons or in the right attitude) whatever it is that the passage in view requires.

2. That is to say, the preacher must always discover the relevance of the death and resurrection of Christ to whatever it is that he is teaching (cf. Phil. 2, for instance, to see how Paul does this). The light of the cross falls across the whole Bible and illumines it all; no passage in Old or New Testament can be preached properly without understanding and explaining how its message relates to the gospel. That is why some are able to find the gospel everywhere—it *is* everywhere! But it does not usually stand alone. Rather, it permeates, fills out, and gives life to every other truth and duty taught in the Scriptures.

Make sure, then, that what you preach is evangel-related (though not always having evangel*ism* as its major thrust). The gospel should be so clear that unbelievers present could be saved (cf. I Cor. 14:23-25). But let the major part of the ministry of the Word be devoted to the proclamation of the whole counsel of God. Christian preaching, within the body, should consist of *the whole counsel of God taught redemptively!* As you study the Scripture, you will discover *that* is the biblical balance in preaching.

7

PREACHING THE GOSPEL IN THE CHURCH

I am not concerned here with evangelistic preaching, so-called. My concern is with the sort of edificational preaching that goes on every Sunday in Bible-teaching churches of the Lord Jesus Christ. Of course, the gospel never can be preached without also having evangelism in view. But the sort of evangelism that takes place in the regular gathering of the people of God will be that kind of evangelism that Paul mentions in I Corinthians 14:23-25—*incidental* evangelism.

What I am talking about is the way in which the letters of the New Testament are written by *preachers,* whose preaching style and content are plainly apparent in them. These books were written to Christian churches and to saved individuals; that means that the purpose of these books was not strictly evangelistic. They dealt with such themes as heresy, schism, lack of love, encouragement, truth: matters you discuss with believers. But—and here is the main point—no matter what the main thrust of any discussion may have been, always the argument, the truth, the exhortation, was presented by Paul, by Peter, or by John *in the light of the gospel.*

When, for instance, Paul wants his readers to change their way of life, he doesn't just say, "get with it, brothers and sisters"; no, he writes:

> I urge you to walk in a way that is appropriate to the calling to which you were called (Eph. 4:1b).

That calling was the great salvation about which he had been writing once again in chapters 1 to 3.

Over and over again in such passages, one encounters both explicit and oblique references to the substitutional, penal, sacrificial death of Christ and to His bodily resurrection. This gospel message seems never to be forgotten. On the contrary, it is always in the writer's mind; he sees all issues in the light of the cross.

This does not mean that Paul preached/wrote about nothing else but the gospel. No, that is exactly not the case. Some preachers fail precisely because that is what they do. They seem to know nothing else. New Testament preachers had much to say about many other topics as well, but everything that they wrote (unlike so much preaching today) was evangelical (gospel oriented) but not strictly evangelistic (i.e., *only* a preaching of the gospel). In other words, all sorts of topics were considered, but whatever was said about a topic could not just as well have been said by an unconverted Jew. Every sermon was distinctively Christian.

That is what I was talking about in the previous essay, on *balance* in preaching. But now, let me ask, How does one preach about other matters in the light of the gospel? In response let me emphasize two things:

1. It is not done by tacking the gospel onto an otherwise gospelless message. That is decidedly not what I have in mind. To preach the gospel at the conclusion of a sermon that otherwise would be acceptable in a synagog may be better than doing nothing at all, but it is not a biblical sort of preaching.
2. It is done, rather, by permeating one's thinking and speaking with the gospel and its implications for the subject being discussed. In preparing the message, the preacher examines all of the relationships of his subject and the gospel and then brings out some of these in the message. In the background of all that he says is a prevailing gospel flavor, or viewpoint that influences the choice of vocabulary, incidental (but important) remarks, the stance toward the subject he takes, etc.

But, in a concrete way, just exactly what does that mean? It means that the area under consideration is related, first, to our sin and failure and our need of a Savior. Apart from the bad news, the gospel is not good news at all. It means also that the subject is related to the gospel itself. The redemption of Jesus Christ is considered in its effect on whatever it is that one is discussing. One considers how Christ forgives, how He changes our sinful desires and turns our interests to serving God, and how He enables us to live differently in the future. In one way or another, all of these things are concerns that rather directly relate to the gospel and form a basis for preaching that is truly evangelical. And they all focus on the power of Christ's liberating death and resurrection. What I am saying is that sanctification ought to be related to justification in preaching, just as it is everywhere in the New Testament. Otherwise, preaching tends to become moralistic.

Let us see how Paul did it. In Ephesians 5:22-33, there is a discussion of the relationship of a husband to his wife. Here the role of each is spelled out—in a redemptive way. The entire passage is thought of in terms of Christ's justifying (v. 25) and sanctifying (vv. 26, 27) relationship to what is called His bride, the church. The work of Christ in redeeming His church, and His present work in relationship to her, are both set forth evangelically. "Be self-sacrificing and kind" is a message that could be preached from a liberal pulpit or in a synagog. That is not Paul's word to husbands. On the contrary, his message is, "Be to your wife all that Christ is to His church. Give yourself to her as Christ gave Himself up for His church." Between the two, there is all the difference in the world. And, added to that is always, in one way or another, the message that you cannot do this yourself, but that by the wisdom and the power of the Holy Spirit who dwells within you, you can.

How do you preach Christ from the Old Testament? By showing how every Old Testament topic relates to the gospel. Be sure that in *all* your preaching—from the Old Testament and from the New—Christ and His death and resurrection condition everything else that you say. Really, in Christian preaching how could it be otherwise? Apart from the gospel, all else is worthless. All is lost. There is no hope, no incentive, no gratitude, no power—nothing! Well, then, if you believe that, preach as if you think it is true. Let your congregation never forget that, regardless of what the topic might be, it holds meaning and significance only in the light of the gospel. And if there is any unbeliever present, it should be possible for him somewhere in every sermon you preach to learn the good news that

> Christ died for our sins according to the Scriptures, and that He was buried and that He was raised on the third day, according to the Scriptures (I Cor. 15:3, 4).

8
SOME NEGLECTED SUBJECTS

The efforts that I have exerted in trying to get pastors of Bible-believing churches to become practical in their use of the Scriptures, and in attempting to get them to speak about subjects that in a previous period were neglected, may have had some influence in turning the preaching of the pulpit around. It is incumbent on me, therefore, to do whatever I can to stop what I perceive to be an unwarranted retreat from the doctrinal teaching that is also a necessary part of the Christian's weekly pulpit diet.

It has been a long time, for instance, since I have heard sermons on the Bible's teaching about hell, judgment, wrath, and other such themes. "You travel in the wrong circles," you may reply. Well, perhaps. But my circles are rather wide, and I hear a lot of preaching. I did not say that it was extinct, but I do think that preaching on these topics is being neglected. The dark side of things is taking a back seat to many of the brighter truths of Scripture. While it is wrong to neglect the latter as a previous generation did, it is also wrong to neglect the former. The biblical balance between the two must always be maintained.

The problem in the church historically has been a problem of balance. The problem is not in the Scriptures—there you will find a perfect balance in every area that is treated by its divinely inspired authors. No, the problem isn't in the Bible; it is in the church. The history of the church could almost be written in terms of swings from one unbiblical extreme to the other. In one era love is emphasized over truth to the extent that truth is lost and love becomes nothing more than sticky sentimental nonsense. In another era, the opposite problem appears—usually as a reaction to the overemphasis of the former age: truth becomes the great concern, so great that love is stamped out in the pursuit of error. In the attempt to flush out every vestige of error hiding in the bushes, theological bloodhounds usurp the authority of the judgment angels whose appointed task is to separate the wheat from the tares. Certainly error must be dealt with—but in biblical ways; we do not have any right to invent novel ways of doing so.

The problem today seems to be a turning from the sterner teachings of the Scriptures to the more encouraging and happier ones. This is proceeding apace; preachers like to preach positively; people like to hear it. While teaching the latter, it is essential to maintain the former as well. Mount Gerazim, with its blessings, was paired in balance with Mount Ebal and its cursings; the tree of life was set over against the tree of the knowledge of good and evil. God is the God of perfect balance; we must seek to approximate Him in this in all our preaching.

Along with extremes comes another problem. When a generation plummets headlong in one direction, heedless of the balancing truths in the other direction, all sorts of false ideas, imported from the outside, seemingly (but not really) saying the same thing are bought and sold as if they were the genuine biblical article. It is easy to do this because the correctives inherent in the neglected balancing truths are missing. That is why the increased concern for teaching about the image of God in man (to the exclusion of preaching about man's sinful nature and propensities) by so many has been wedded to many false concepts gleaned from psychologists like Maslow and others concerning self-image and self-worth. In discussions of the area, the doctrine of sanctification has been eclipsed by the doctrine of justification (for more on this, cf. John Bettler's tapes on the subject of self-image, available from Christian Study Services, 1790 E. Willow Grove Avenue, Laverock, PA 19118).

"Surely I'm not guilty of an overemphasis on the happy side of the faith to the near exclusion of the grim side," you may reply. Don't be too sure. Check out your preaching for the past three years; you may be surprised at what you find. You may discover that the emphasis of the era in which you are living has had a greater impact on your ministry than you realize. At any rate, even if you are one of those rare, balanced persons who preach away year after year, unaffected by the changing extremes all around them, it will not hurt you to do the examination anyway, since it will give you a greater perspective on the sort of emphases that you need to make over the next year or two.

It is a good policy to plan broad sweeps of preaching anyway, so that you may stay in balance. And, even you, balanced as you may be, are a sinner who—if you are honest—must admit that you tend to ride your *own* hobbies to the neglect of biblical truths that balance. I dare you to try doing a three-year study without finding some!

9

USING THE ORIGINAL LANGUAGES IN PREACHING

"Why do I need to? After all, there was no time in the history of preaching when there were more good translations than now."

The argument *sounds* good; but the objector misses the obvious fact that the more translation possibilities that he has to choose from, the more one needs to know (at least *something* about) the original languages; otherwise, when they differ (and they do), how does he know which is correct? From which should he preach? Which more faithfully represents the original text of the writers? This is a special problem today, when so many translators have determined to become interpretive in their renderings. The very wealth of modern options itself should (all the more) point up the need for an acquaintance with the original languages. Without some such knowledge of the orginal languages, how will you be able to evaluate them?

"Where can I get this knowledge?" Self-help books and taped language courses in both Greek and Hebrew exist. But (easiest) many Bible colleges, all conservative seminaries, and a number of other schools provide courses in the original languages. Any pastor who has never had Greek or Hebrew (even if he doesn't ever complete a seminary education) ought to take these courses.

"Why?" Well, not only to decide between translations, but:

1. To be able to "get the feel" of a passage. English translations tend to trowel off the original tone of the writers. Only by becoming acquainted with the original can one restore this. This "feel" is essential to good preaching.
2. To be able to use the best commentaries and read the better Bible helps (most of which refer to the original text). Without some knowledge of the languages, one cannot follow the reasoning behind the renderings suggested.
3. To be able to evaluate other books whose authors (again, *not* using

the original) may be far afield in their interpretations and/or uses of many passages.

4. Preaching that flows from the study of a passage in the original moves forward with a more sure-footed stride; other preaching often limps. A certain confidence derives from having examined the text for one's self. On the other hand, knowing the exegetical difficulties in a preaching portion may deter one from rushing ahead when he ought to tread more cautiously.

"But I'll never be a Greek or Hebrew scholar." Right! That is true of most pastors. And right there lies the problem. Many good men who could have profited from a sensible use of the original languages were turned off by seminary teachers who taught them the study of languages as if their life occupation would be to teach classics or semitics in a university. They never recommended shortcuts (e.g., like forgetting all about the rules for Greek accents—learning these is an almost totally unnecessary chore. One can get along well with learning only those distinguishing accents that count). They tried to build up a conscience against using analytical lexicons and interlinear translations (two *very* valuable helps that no one should feel guilty about using freely). They talk negatively about such books as Kubo's *Reader's Lexicon* and don't tell students about Spiro Zodiates' crib for Machen's grammar. All such "purism" is sheer nonsense. Who cares if a pastor leans on some Bagster help? Who cares *how* a minister learns to get the right answers to his exegetical questions concerning the original languages, so long as he gets them? After all, I'm not advocating anything immoral, unethical or unbiblical! Of course one should use the *Englishman's Hebrew and Chaldee Concordance* and *Wilson's O.T. Word Studies* (a book I find invaluable) if he finds them helpful. Why not?

With all that a busy pastor must do, it is only right for him to employ every available aid that he can afford, to keep his hand into the continued use of Hebrew and Greek. He would be a poor steward of time and energy if he did not. Many men have *lost* any language ability they once had because they believed (what they were told, or strongly led to think) that it was wrong to use anything but the naked text and the standard grammars and lexicons. Sheer, unadulterated nonsense! Pastor, if using an interlinear will help you get back to the

Greek and Hebrew, use it—let me emancipate you from the chains of guilt forged in the shops of language teachers who never had to face the everyday problems of the pastorate. Use it! Use whatever is available. Indeed, every teacher of Hebrew and Greek in a theological seminary ought to take the time to compare and contrast these helps, giving his opinion about which is best (and why) and instructing pastors in the most effective and intelligent use of each.

Preach; preach from a study of the original text, using all the helps you can get your hands on, and you will preach with confidence and joy.

10

ADAPTATION THROUGH AUDIENCE ANALYSIS

You cannot preach to everyone in exactly the same way and expect your preaching to be effective. Paul and Peter didn't; neither may you.[1] Yet, regardless of the occasion—whether at the young people's hot dog roast or at the funeral of an elder in the congregation, some preachers sound exactly the same.

There is no variation in the content, the length, the vocabulary, the tone of voice, or the form of the message that they present. What that means, in the final analysis, is that there is an inadequate concern for people or for the God who called us to minister to them. The essence of professionalism is a focus on one's self and an implicit demand that others adapt and conform to our ways. The essence of servanthood and ministry, on the other hand, is a concern for those to whom one is ministering, a desire to please the One who called us to minister and, therefore, a willingness to adapt in whatever ways we legitimately can to serve better than before.

Adaptation is not accommodation. The two are opposites. The accommodator changes God's message to conform to the listener, to the speaker, or to both. There is concern about people, but it is a humanistic and unbiblical concern that overrides concern for God. And it is a concern that, in the final analysis, is superficial and often ingenuine. This concern to accommodate truth often amounts to little more than a concern for one's self—what others will think of me. True concern for others will push self into the background while concentrating on what is best for them; it will cause one to speak "in season" (when the results are likely to enhance relationships) and *out of season* (when they are not). It will impel him to speak hard things for the benefit of others when necessary, even at his own peril.

---

1. Cf. my book, *Audience Adaptation in the Sermons and Speeches of Paul.*

While accommodation is self-centered (or, at its best, humanistically oriented toward others), adaptation is other-concerned. The speaker who takes the time to adapt his message doesn't change the message at all; he changes his own ways and in every circumstance adopts the best possible method of conveying that message to others. He changes *himself,* not the message; he, himself, becomes flexible and moldable *in order to meet each situation and/or group of persons to whom he is speaking.* He is the one who moves—he is willing to discover where his audience is and to travel to that spot. Unlike the professional, he does not expect his audience to make all of the movement toward him.

But how does he do this? Much could be said in response to that question, but I should like to mention only two (crucial) points. Successful adaptation involves:

1. A willingness to develop several styles and an ability to move with agility from one to another.
2. An ability to analyze audiences and circumstances in order to determine how best to adapt one's style to them.

Both of these speaking skills are implied in Paul's words when he wrote:

> Don't be a cause for stumbling to Jews or to Greeks or to God's church;[2] just as I please all sorts of people in all sorts of matters, not seeking my own advantage but rather the advantage of many so that they may be saved (I Cor. 10:32, 33).

He was making the same point a chapter earlier:

> To Jews, I became like a Jew so that I might win Jews; to those who are under the law I became like one who is under the law (although I myself am not under law), so that I might win those who are under law; to those without law I became like one who is without law (although I am not without God's law, but within Christ's law) so that I might win those who are without law (I Cor. 9:20, 21).

In these words several things are apparent:

1. Paul's concern for others rather than himself (he was keenly aware

---

[2] I.e., either in your evangelism (to Jews and Greeks) or in your edification (God's church) of others. Adaptation applies *to both.*

of the problem as I stated it earlier). Note his words about whose "advantage" was to be sought.
2. Paul's willingness to adapt. He was willing to change *himself* (*"To Jews I became,"* etc.); of course he was unwilling to change his message (indeed, he suffered greatly for that unwillingness—cf. II Cor. 6:4-10; 11:23-29).
3. Paul's ability to analyze and adapt (note how he distinguished between audiences: Jews under law, Gentiles not under law, the church within Christ's law).[3]

The willingness to adapt grows out of (1) a recognition of the need to do so and (2) a genuine concern for God's truth and for those to whom one preaches. These are largely matters of attitude and commitment. The abilities to analyze and adapt, however, are skills. These two skills must be developed and practiced until learned.

Mainly, audience analysis takes time and thought. Deep concern for God and for the congregation alone will induce a busy preacher to take the time out of a pressured schedule to do the necessary spade work. That is probably one reason why so little adaptation is done. When thinking analytically about an audience, you ought to ask questions like these:

1. How much do they know about the message?
2. What, if any, are some misconceptions and/or prejudices that they may hold?
3. What are some of the obstacles that may intrude in:
    a. communicating the message,
    b. persuading people of its truth, and/or
    c. motivating them to act on it?
4. Are there any reasons why I might turn them off?
5. What technical terms will I need to use and to explain?
6. How would I best illustrate the truth to *this* group?
    a. What are the best areas from which to draw illustrations?
    b. What sort of language should I use with this group to make my illustrations clear?

---

3. These distinctions went much further, as a study of his speeches and sermons in the Book of Acts shows. In no two messages does he use exactly the same approach. The message is constant; the method varies.

7. What do I need to say in order to demonstrate how to implement the action(s) required?
8. Is the audience varied enough in the above matters that I shall have to approach the question from more than one angle?
9. Given the general spiritual condition of the congregation, how much truth can I communicate, and to what depth?
10. Is my problem with this group fundamentally to give them information, to persuade them to believe or disbelieve something (or both), or to get them to *do* what they already know and believe? Or is it a combination of two or more of the above?

These are not the only questions to ask, but they will give you a good start on audience analysis if you will use them. For the next six months, each week as you work on your messages, ask them. They, in turn, will lead to further considerations. Answers will not always come immediately, but as you continue to adapt your proclamation of truth regularly you will discover that they will come with increasing rapidity and that not only will you soon be arriving at a profusion of answers but, on top of that, you will find that you are beginning to enjoy the adaptation process.[4]

---

4. For more on adaptation in ministry, see my book, *Insight and Creativity*.

11

PREACHING AND WRITING

Many of the great preachers—Spurgeon, Luther, Calvin, etc. (not to mention Paul, Peter, and John)—also have been great writers. Certainly, there are exceptions, but, on the whole, the observation holds. Why is that?

Perhaps there are numerous other factors involved in this phenomenon, but one that we should not miss is that writing helps preaching (as, doubtless, preaching helps writing). It is that observation to which I now wish to direct your attention.

Years ago Andrew Blackwood pointed out this relationship between writing and preaching to us in his classes. At the time, while I respected many of his views, I was not sure that this one was correct. Now, after many years of preaching, teaching preaching, and writing, I want to take my place at his side and declare to all who will listen, "Blackwood was right! If you want to preach well, write."

Let me share with you some of the ways in which writing has helped me become a more effective preacher.

First, writing demands accuracy and precision. When these things are missing in a sermon, it is easier for both the preacher and his congregation to overlook the fact. You can slip so much by yourself and the congregation because much depends on voice and body. In writing, however, one reads and rereads, in a critical manner, what he has written, correcting errors and demanding of his work more and more intelligibility because he knows words must do it all. He does in written material what it is much more difficult to do in preaching: because preaching is live, the preacher cannot go back and edit what he has said the way that a writer can. Nor can he let the sermon sit until another day and look at it from the perspective of all the new horizons of thought and emotion that that day brings (it is utterly amazing what a fresh look at a manuscript several days later can do for it). So, in general, the mere ability to reread and rewrite after a time as one subjects his own thought to heavy scrutiny itself is a powerful incentive to improve.

Because the preacher who does not write is denied this discipline of self-criticism (criticizing a sermon, even with the use of a tape recorder, is still difficult and is a very different thing[1]), he is not as likely to change his style and grammar as the one who regularly writes.

It is not important what one writes, so long as he develops the habit of self-criticism. One of the greatest failures of poor preachers is their failure to revise. He could be writing for his denominational paper, for his church newsletter, or for a publisher. In each case, if he is highly critical of his own work, using the eraser frequently, trying on new ways of saying things for size, always improving on what he has done, he will find in time the experiments and discoveries made in writing will bleed over into his preaching. Usually, he will not even have to make the transition in any conscious way.

Let's take an example. For some time, I had been aware of an archaic sound in the King James Version that frequently had not been removed from a number of modern versions. But I just couldn't put my finger on what it was. Then as I began to translate the New Testament for myself (a writing task), I discovered what it was: an archaic use of the word "for." This use of "for" may be good current British English, but it is certain that it has long since passed out of American English. Its continued use in translating the Greek word *gar* made these modern translations sound stilted and somewhat less than modern in many places. Take, for instance, Luke 1:13 (one instance of thousands): "Do not be afraid, Zacharias, for your petition has been heard. . . ." In modern English, we in America would use a semicolon instead of the word "for": Do not be afraid, Zacharias; your prayer has been heard." The ancient "for" and the modern semicolon serve exactly the same purpose. In other places, as in Luke 1:15,18, where the word opens a new sentence, it is better in translating to omit the "for" altogether.

If I hadn't been involved in a writing endeavor, I might never have discovered what it was that made otherwise modern translations sound somewhat less modern. Many of the smaller subtleties like

---

1. I am assuming that sermons are not delivered from a full manuscript.

this will come to light only as one takes upon himself the task of creating meaning in sentences that are put on paper, examined and altered in order to make them more intelligible and acceptable to the modern ear. It is probably because they don't write that so many preachers perpetrate the same old errors and archaisms that their fathers and forefathers did. It is amazing what vitality these ancient inhibitors to communication show when they are allowed to thrive in an environment free from any blue-penciling.

But there are other ways in which writing helps one to improve his preaching. The combination of hand and eye and subvocal speech (good preachers always sound out what they write to discover for themselves how it is likely to come across to the reader) impresses new and better ways of communicating on the writer-preacher by means of three—not one—avenues; and he remembers them because a threefold cord isn't easily broken.

But most of all, the writing process is, by the nature of its demand, the one discipline in which the preacher can regularly engage that will bring about improvements to his grammar, syntax, and style. Without some *regular* incentive to look up the *exact* meaning of words, as one is much more likely to do in writing than when he must do so *after* the sermon is over (you can't carry a dictionary into the pulpit to use whenever you aren't absolutely sure of the precise usage of a term[2]), few of us will do it. Without some necessity to think about grammar and style, who will do it on his own? We are busy people in the ministry, and we know well that we will allow such matters to slide unless *forced* to do otherwise. So, if for no other reason, writing is helpful because it requires the preacher to think about the tools that he uses in his trade, and makes it much more likely that he will take better care of them.

Let me ask you—how well do you use these tools? If you don't regularly write something, somewhere, your language will rust. Be honest—did someone leave your church recently because he was tired of hearing your vocabulary squeak and grind?

---

2. Incidentally, do you read the dictionary regularly? "Read the dictionary regularly—isn't that like reading the telephone directory?" No, it isn't. You can learn a great deal, discover many good sermon illustrations, and sharpen your understanding and subsequent use of words by just reading the dictionary from A to Z. P.S. If you have trouble going to sleep, it's also a good book to read in bed at night.

12

MAKING PREACHING A PLEASURE

Most pastors enjoy preaching. Moreover, many thoroughly enjoy the hours of preparation spent in the study among their commentaries and other books in the work of biblical exposition and sermon preparation. Why, then, do we hear so much dissatisfaction about preaching from preachers themselves these days?

The basic dissatisfaction, about which I am speaking, is the outgrowth of another problem stemming (in turn) from still another.

First, dissatisfaction comes from not "having enough time" to prepare properly. It is precisely the opportunity to study and prepare sermons that pastors enjoy so much that is lacking. They *want* to spend more time in the study of the Word and in the preparation of messages, but other demands constantly call them away from this work. Doing half-baked study and inadequate preparation is what takes away the joy of preaching. That's the first problem.

But before going on to the second problem (from which it derives), let's consider this matter of the lack of time a bit more thoroughly. Perhaps you are expecting me to say, "Well, if you're too busy to find time, then you're just too busy." There is something to that, of course. Any number of preachers take on tasks that do not belong to them; disregarding the clear statement of their function in Ephesians 4:11, 12, they try to do the work of their people for them, in addition to all their own. That, of course, is impossible. Some pastors run a taxi service, mow lawns, operate mimeograph machines, etc., when there are any number of persons in the congregation who could (should) do these things instead. When they arrogate to themselves the tasks that others ought to do, but are not doing, they make it easy for others to shirk their responsibilities, they rob them of their blessings, and they crowd out the study of Scripture and sermon preparation. It ought to be a rule for every pastor not to do anything himself that a member of his congregation can do (or can be taught to do) as well as (or better than) himself. Of course, there will be times (in emergencies, in brand new mission churches, etc.) when a pastor must do such things, but he will not make it a practice. His work is ministering the Word, privately and publicly, in order to build up and encourage all the members of the flock to discover, undertake, and engage in their own ministries. When *extraneous* activities are eliminated from his schedule, he will have more time for study and sermon preparation.

"But that isn't all," you say. Right! I know there are weeks that we'd all like to forget; and I know that they come more frequently than we'd like to think. On Monday it looks tight (especially with that special men's meeting address on Saturday night), but everything seems to be in hand. You have selected your preaching portions for Sunday morning and evening and the prayer meeting topic, and you are about to go to work on them (Saturday night will have to wait till Thursday). You are well into your exegesis by Tuesday morning, when things begin to break loose. The phone—that two-faced blessing and curse—rings. Mrs. Green has been rushed to the hospital . . . it is serious . . . can you come immediately? You do, of course (torn at leaving the study at such a time). When you get back (three hours later), there is the afternoon's list of activities staring you in the face. No way for you to fudge on them. So, you don't. That means one half of a morning's study shot. "I'll catch up tonight," you think, as you drive out of the yard. But that night finds you at the hospital again—Mrs. Green has taken a turn for worse; they think she may die. Somehow, she rallies, and you go home late, weary, but no further ahead in your study. Wednesday morning. Sunday sermons are set aside. Tonight's prayer meeting must be considered. "I'll take off this afternoon and do the study I had hoped to do yesterday. Who is that driving up to the study? Bill and Jane Wilkes. Wonder what they want?" It turns out that last night Jane threatened to leave Bill, and only at the last minute was she persuaded to stay *on condition that they see the pastor right away*. "Of course," you hear yourself saying, "sit down; let's talk about it." Glad to help, but reluctant to give up the time, you counsel them. When you are through, an hour and a half later, your secretary informs you that this *really* looks like it for Mrs. Green—and that the family would like to see you (they have all gathered together at the hospital). You go (of course!). Mrs. Green dies (this means another unanticipated message for Saturday morning at the funeral). Bill and Jane take up another day or two—and so it goes (I'll not finish out the week—it's too discouraging to do so). I know about those kinds of weeks—and what they can do to sermon preparation and study.

"Well?" you ask. "What can I do about that sort of problem? There isn't any way that you can regulate funerals, marriages breaking up, etc., so that they fit your study schedule, is there?" Don't be too sure! While you can't predict emergencies, you may be able to regulate your schedule to fit emergencies in a way that doesn't destroy your study and preparation.

I am about to make a suggestion that at first you will reject—but hear me out. In one fell swoop you can solve not only the problem of weekly pressure, but a number of other problems as well. Indeed, following this suggestion can—as it did for me in my last pastorate—make preaching a pleasure.

The suggestion is simple, but profound: prepare every sermon six months in advance. Now wait, don't turn me off. Hear me out, I beg you. I want to make it clear that this is the easiest and the most practical thing to do. Here are my reasons:

In preparing six months in advance,

1. You gain plenty of lead-time that will allow you to make all the schedule adjustments that you need to meet emergencies. What you lose in time one week can be gained the next week (or the week after).
2. You gain perspective on your text. Too many sermons are cut down green; they do not have time to ripen.
3. Illustrations come naturally. When you know well in advance what you will be preaching about, all the general reading you do, as well as the experiences you have, feed into the sermon. You don't have to *search* for examples; they *come* to you.
4. When preaching a series of sermons on a book, you can preach the first sermon in the light of the exegesis of the entire book. Instead of discovering that what you preached in the first chapter was wrong (now that you understand it in terms of what is said later in chapter 3), you begin to preach the book only after having studied the whole.

5. You solve the problems of an exegetical conscience. When you begin preparing a message on Monday or Tuesday before it is to be preached, you may move along swimmingly until—in the mail Friday—you receive that new commentary that you ordered that knocks your previous understanding of the passage into the proverbial hat. Now, what do you do? There isn't any time to adequately prepare a *new* sermon. Do you preach the old one, knowing it is wrong? I'm afraid many do.
6. Preachers tend to ride hobbies (Ezekiel at night, Revelation in the morning, and Daniel for prayer meeting). Planning large blocks of sermons, well in advance, requires thought about balanced feeding of the flock.

All in all, then, I think you can see the values of preparing six months in advance.

"Sure, I can see that all right, but I don't see how it can be done."

What you do is this:
1. You do the exegesis for your passage and outline it in rough form six months ahead.
2. You allow time for your thinking about it to mature, in the meantime gathering illustrations, etc.
3. A couple of weeks before preaching you pull out your folder and put the sermon into final form.

Of course, you can always make adjustments in unforeseen circumstances by inserting a special sermon now and then to meet these.

Let me diagram the process:

The Preaching Year

You divide the year (roughly) into four segments, according to some functional form (as suggested above). Then you plan two segments of the year all at one time (e.g., at the end of summer you might plan the spring and summer segments of the following year.

The Preaching Year

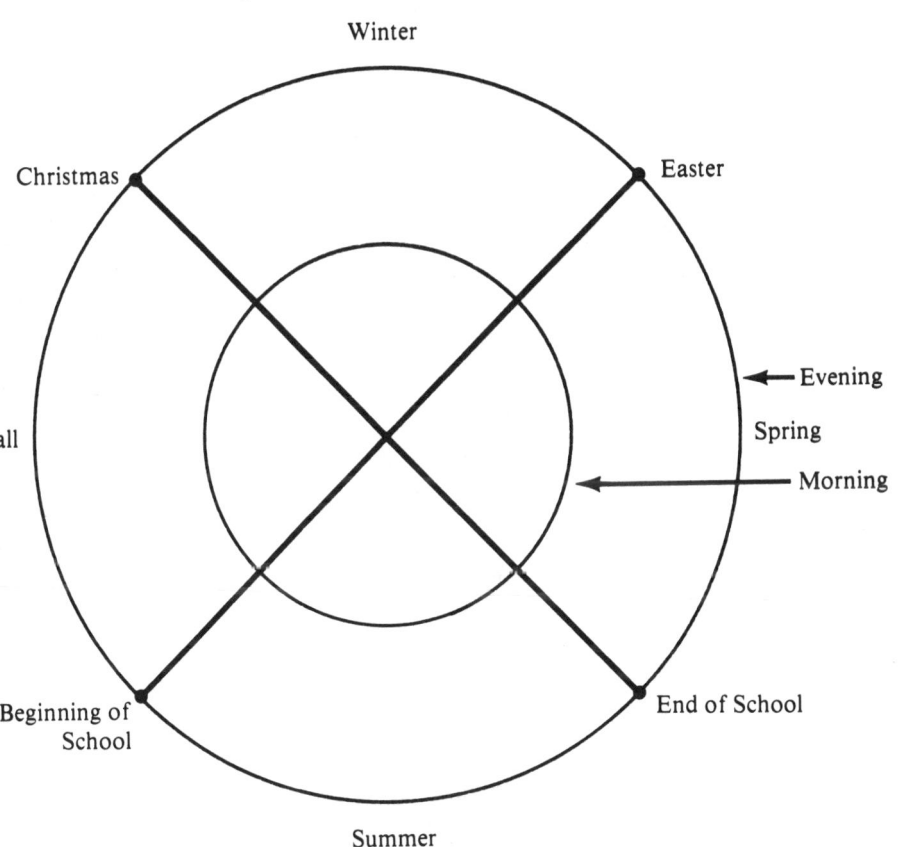

Then you begin studying each of the messages to be preached during those segments, keeping six months ahead. That looks like this:

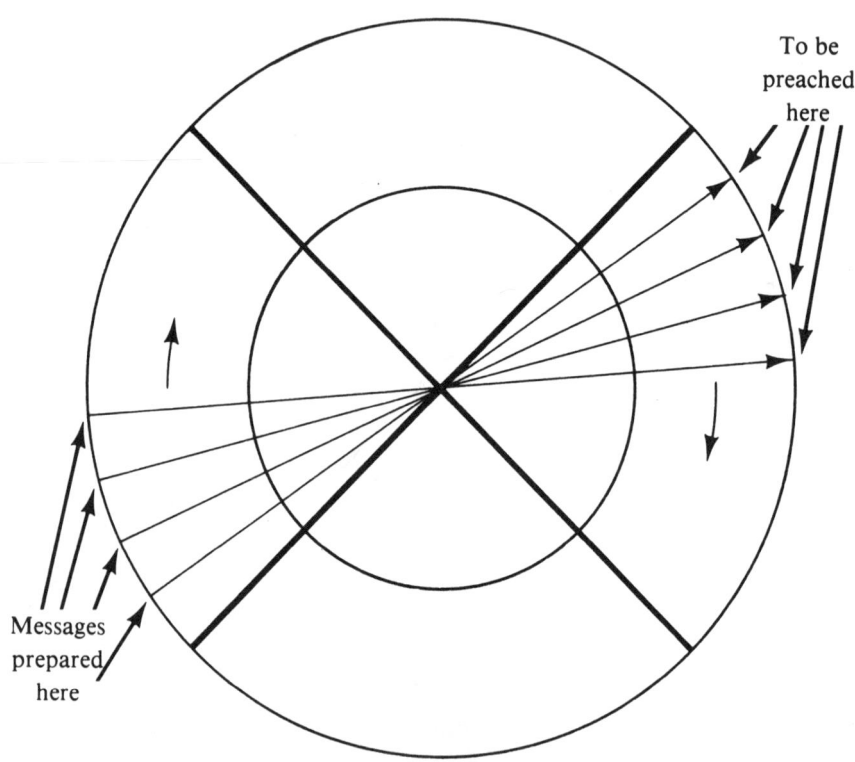

The two segments ahead also can be prepared in balanced terms by using the diagram, thus:

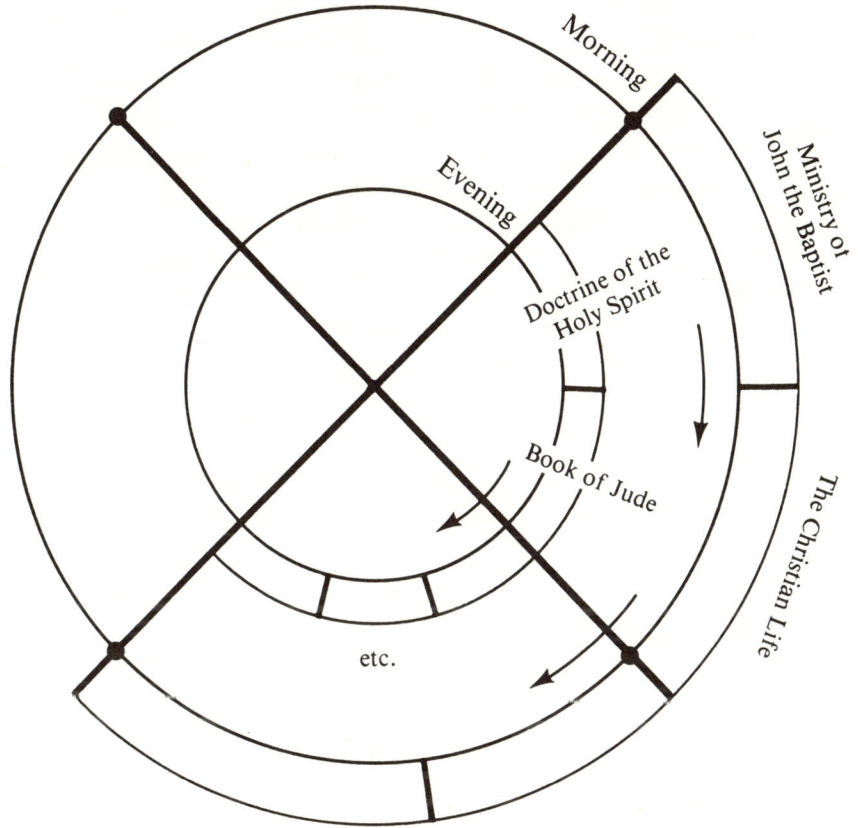

"OK, OK. I can see the value of this. But is it really practical? Can it actually be done? If so, how?"

Let me assure you that it can. I did it myself and have helped any number of other pastors to do so too. They too report success and joy in using the method. What you are now doing isn't practical, is it? Well then, consider this.

1. The best time to make the change is when changing pastorates. Simply preach out of the barrel for six months while preparing the next six. A sermon is best preached the third or fourth time!
2. If you are in seminary, determine not to leave with less than six months' sermons in hand. Start out right from the beginning.

3. If you are in a pastorate, and intend to stay, but want to switch over to the new program, I suggest this:
   a. Dig into the barrel for your oldest, very first sermons.
   b. Develop six months worth of sermons from these.
   c. Use each major point of these as a separate sermon in itself. (Typically, new preachers include too much in their sermons. When you preach these points separately, you will have the sermon you should have had to begin with.)

I have outlined a process and procedure that can revolutionize your preaching. Don't lay it aside lightly. I have suggested this to any number of persons. Those who have adopted it agree that they have been liberated. Preaching can be the pleasure you always wanted it to be.

13

OUTLINING

More strange things have been taught concerning outlining than perhaps any other aspect of sermon preparation. In this chapter I hope to set a few of these to rest.

"This text naturally falls into three divisions," says the typical self-styled "expositor." Well, isn't that interesting? So what?

"What do you mean, 'so what?' If it falls into three divisions, then I will be most biblical when I divide my sermon into three parts that correspond to each of these three divisions—that's what!"

Hogwash!

"Hogwash? Do you mean that Jay Adams, the fellow who is always talking about being biblical, doesn't believe you should allow the text itself to determine the outline? I can hardly believe that!"

Well, it's true! And I'll tell you why—because it is unbiblical to do so!

"You'll have to explain that one to me—and it'd better be good!"

OK. Let's begin by pointing out that nowhere—and I mean *nowhere*—in the New Testament (or Old Testament, for that matter) does anyone preach a sermon that way. No one ever dreamed of it until many years later, when the scholastics invented the method, with which we have been plagued ever since. Can you imagine Peter on the day of Pentecost getting up and saying, "Now this text from Joel naturally falls into, . . ." or something comparable? Not on your life! Neither Peter, nor Stephen, nor Paul, nor any other speaker or writer does any such thing. It simply isn't biblical to do so.

Think with me about this approach. To observe that a passage falls into so many natural divisions may be of importance *as a literary analysis* that may help in interpreting or understanding it. But how a passage naturally divides is no guideline for construction of the preacher's sermon. Such an analysis, for instance, may reveal that there are two divisions of a proverb or in a verse of a psalm. But what does that mean? It probably means that you will be preaching from Hebrew poetry, which is constructed in parallel form. Does that indicate that every sermon you preach from Proverbs will be two-pointed?

Actually, the Bible is constructed out of a number of distinct kinds of literature, each of which has its own peculiar form. There is the poetic parallelism (synthetic, complementing, contrasting, etc.) already mentioned, biography, narrative, proverb (akin to poetry, but with its own twist), parable, the letter, apocalyptic (some built around the number 7; does that mean nothing but seven-pointed sermons from Revelation? Heaven forbid!), the sermon,[1] and so on. Each type of literature has its own style.

That means that when you tell a congregation your text "falls naturally into . . . parts," you are simply giving them the results of a literary analysis. Interesting, perhaps, but it isn't preaching.

Why do you think that the form of a *sermon* should be determined by a narrative or a poetical form? You are not going to tell a story or recite a poem; you are going to preach. Preaching demands its own form, just as truly as parable or poetry. Like all of the preachers in the New Testament, you too must "translate" the particular form of your preaching portion into a preaching form. A proverb may fall naturally into two divisions, but your sermon from that proverb may best take a fourfold form.

It is true that in some of Paul's writings the preacher does well with the scholastic approach of dividing the passage into its natural parts—but why? Because Paul—above all else—was a preacher of the Word (though he *never* used the "it falls naturally into . . ." method). And, as such, when he dictated his letters to an amanuensis, he often preached in those letters. So, many Pauline passages naturally lend themselves to preaching since they are already virtually in preaching form.[2] But that certainly isn't true of all, or even most, biblical writing. Acrostic psalms (like the 119th) took their form for easier memorizing. But when you preach, you are not conducting a course in Bible memory (of course with a sermon *good* alliteration, for instance, can aid in remembering—e.g., "mutual ministry," "marriage is a covenant of companionship"), you are preaching! That is why I say that to be biblical, you must not simply give a literary analysis of the text. Rather, the sermon takes its form from a combina-

---

1. It is the sermonic form in the Bible that we must master. These were used by biblical preachers who translated other types of material into a preaching form.
2. And from them we must learn much about preaching form.

tion of the content, the occasion, and the audience (for more on this, see volume 2 of my *Studies in Preaching: Audience Adaptation in the Sermons and Speeches of Paul*).

Now let me move on to another matter. You will need to develop a preaching stance to which your sermon outline will correspond.

The "This passage naturally falls into . . ." approach grows out of a non-preaching stance toward the Bible and toward the congregation. It comes from the ivy-covered halls of isolated scholars; not from the work-a-day studies of pastors. Such scholarship is necessary to help us analyze and understand a passage; but it should not be carried into the pulpit.

Much of what goes for preaching week by week bears only a dim and distant resemblance to true preaching. Instead, it more closely resembles the lecture format by which aspiring young theologs almost exclusively are trained in seminaries. It may be fine for theological halls (at times), but it is not fine for the pulpit—IT IS NOT PREACHING!

Let me compare and contrast what I call a *lecture stance* with a *preaching stance*. A lecture stance stresses the long-ago-and-far-away (what happened to those Israelites, or David, or Solomon), it predominantly uses the past tense, speaks in the third person, talks *about* the Bible, is abstract, and—in its best form—tacks on an application at the end. A preaching stance, however, stresses the here-and-now (what the passage says to the congregation about *their* lives), predominantly uses the present and future tenses, speaks in the second person, and preaches concretely from the Bible about the congregation in relationship to God and neighbor. Let me try to put this another way.

<u>PREACHING STANCE</u>

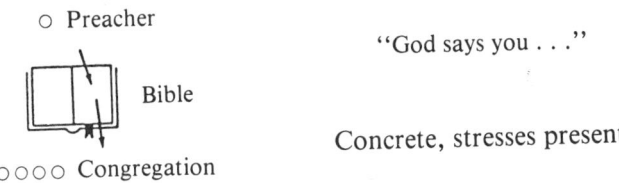

In the preaching stance, the congregation is addressed directly from the Bible. The preacher says, "*God says you. . . .*"

LECTURE STANCE

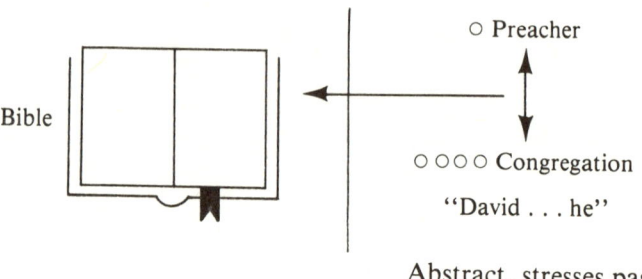

Abstract, stresses past

In the lecture stance, the preacher talks to the congregation about the Bible and what happened way-back-when. He says, "David . . . he,"

"But don't you miss the biblical exposition in doing this?" No, no; a thousand times no! There is no less exposition of the text. All that happened to David (Paul, etc.) is brought out just as fully as in the lecture method. But it is brought out *differently;* not as abstract fact (which may or may not be applied if and when the preacher gets around to it). No! It is brought out *from the outset in relationship to the hearer.* The *whole* sermon (even when explaining what God did for Abraham) then is application. The preacher begins not with the text (explaining it without giving the listener the slightest hint about its relevance to him), but with the congregation. First, he raises some issue for them (by direct question, "Have you wondered why your teenagers are so hard to handle today?," by story, "Last year in a town not many miles from here. . . ." etc.). *Then,* having caught their attention, raised their concern, etc. (i.e., having gotten them *involved* in the subject), he turns to the text and says something like this: "Well, then, if you are concerned about what God says to do about this matter, turn with me to Ephesians 6:4, where we read. . . ."

In harmony with the preaching stance, the congregation brings its interested concerns to the text from the outset, expectantly waiting for God to speak to their problem from it, *instead of merely analyzing scriptural passages!* All that David or Solomon did and what God did for them is taught *just as fully* as in the lecture stance; but it is taught *in order to meet the congregation's present-day concerns*. The Bible becomes a vital Book dealing with their lives *today*. They know this, are personally oriented toward the text from the outset, and therefore look at the passage in an involved way from the outset.

Corresponding to this approach is the concrete, personal outline of the preacher in contrast to the abstract, impersonal outline of the lecturer who (in the name of expository preaching) does a literary and historical analysis of the passage. Contrast the two (oversimplified) outlines:

LECTURE OUTLINE
I. The Duty of Intercessory Prayer
II. The Purpose of Intercessory Prayer
III. The Results of Intercessory Prayer

PREACHING OUTLINE
I. God commands you to *pray* for others
II. God commands you to pray for *others*
III. God commands you to pray for others' *needs*

The outlines above cover roughly the same material. But the first is analytical; it discusses the "nature" of intercessory prayer. The second is motivational; it discusses God's command to the congregation to pray for others. Do you see the difference?

As a *very* helpful exercise, go back through a number of your past sermon outlines and (1) notice how many are abstract; (2) translate them into preaching outlines by concretizing (get rid of abstractions like duty, purpose, results, nature, etc.) and personalizing (add "you" to each point[3]). On the use of the second person go through the

---

3. In many instances, you could preach the sermon again, from the new stance, and most of the members of the congregation wouldn't know it (you'd have to change the illustrations, of course, since they would remember these).

sermons in Acts and underline all the uses of the second person. You will quickly see how frequently the New Testament preachers preached *personally to the members of the audience about their relationship to God*, rather than simply stating objective facts. They preached the Bible, not about the Bible.

Following the simple advice in this article could *transform* your preaching; it did mine. And I have known a large number of preachers who, having caught on to it, have discovered that they too began to preach with results as never before.

14
DON'T TELL US WHAT YOU ARE GOING TO DO—DO IT

I have been noting a tendency among preachers that is common enough to warrant a label; I have called it *prefacing*. Prefacing is the bad habit of announcing what one is about to do before doing it, *when there is no reason for doing so* (note the important italicized qualification).

Let me suggest two ways in which prefacing frequently takes place in preaching:
 1. When one announces beforehand the points in his sermon.
 2. When he announces beforehand that he is about to illustrate.

An example of the first is exactly what I did in the previous paragraph. Reread it and you will discover what I am talking about. And to go on to illustrate the second point I could now say, "Let me give you an example of what I am talking about" (of course, as you see, I just did).

But what is wrong with prefacing? When there is no good reason to do so, it breaks the continuity of what one has been saying by calling attention away from the content to the structure by which that content is being presented.

Foolishly, some homileticians have declared that a preacher should announce all of the points in every sermon. Why? Because they said so, that's why. There is no other good reason. No biblical precedent for doing so can be found. Search the Scriptures and you will not find a single instance of anyone announcing, "This morning I should like to tell you three facts about hell" (or whatever). It just doesn't happen. It doesn't happen because it *shouldn't* happen. Such prefacing adds nothing and certainly detracts.

Now, I did mention a qualification. One *should* announce points if, and *only* if, by doing so he furthers content. That is to say, if, for instance, there are "two steps and only two steps" in dealing with a habit pattern (putting off/putting on), and it is important to stress that there are no more and no less, then the steps and their number become a part of the content itself.

That is the *only* time when it is right to announce points: when knowing the points themselves in some way contributes to the discussion. Otherwise, prefacing and announcing distract.

Again, the same principle holds true for announcing the use of examples and illustrations. It is always wrong to do so unless it serves a better purpose than buying time for the speaker to think (that should have been done before entering the pulpit). There *are* times, of course, when calling attention to the fact that one is about to use an example can be useful. Consider this: "The example I am about to use does not *always* apply, nor does it apply to *everyone*. As you listen, then, ask yourself, is this for me?" In a case like this, where it is important for the listener to evaluate what he is about to hear in a certain way, prefacing the example can be useful—indeed, vital.

But most prefacing—of examples, of points in a sermon, of biblical passages about to be read—is filler. One of the things that makes sermons dull and uninviting is filler.

So, from now on let me give you this word of advice. Stop telling us what you are going to do—just do it. Don't announce points, just make them; don't preface examples, just give them—and your sermons will be smoother and more powerful as a result.

15
ILLUSTRATING GOD'S TRUTH

Illustrations are the life blood of a sermon. They create and hold interest, make a point clearer than the mere statement of it ever could, concretize abstract fact, show how to implement biblical requirements, and help make truth practical and memorable. What remarkable service illustrations can render; no wonder Christ used so many of them!

And you will do well to learn how to freely use them too.

"But I have always been weak in illustration; I really don't know how to go about learning to illustrate well. Can anyone with the basic gifts for the ministry learn to illustrate sermons effectively?" Yes. "Can you tell me how to do so?" Again yes. But, first, let me clarify one thing.

I want to say that, in speaking so positively about illustrations, I am not advocating the string-of-pearls sermon. According to those who use the s-o-p method of preparation, *all* one needs to do to produce a sermon is to get the basic theme of a preaching portion and a dozen or more extended illustrations that fit it; those are his basic materials for sermon construction. The message thus becomes little more than a number of illustrations draped along the theme like pearls strung on a necklace. There is little or no exposition, very little reasoning or grappling with truth in it. Rather, what one does is to focus on illustrations rather than on the biblical passage. That is bad news; the authority of the preacher's message comes from a human rather than a divinely inspired source.

No. Every sincere listener should be able to go away from every sermon knowing, at least,

1. What the passage (or passages) dealt with *means;* i.e., he should now understand it even if he didn't before;

2. What the passage means to *him;* i.e., he should know what the Holy Spirit intended that passage to do to him;
3. What he must prayerfully *do* to obey any commands, appropriate any promises, etc; i.e., he should know how to convert the passage into daily life today;
4. That the authority for what the preacher is teaching clearly is *scriptural;* i.e., he should be able to see that the preacher got what he is saying from the passage (or passages) under consideration.

Plainly, if those four elements constitute biblical preaching (and they do) then to be biblical a sermon must be *much* more than a string of pearls!

Yet, within the framework of the four principles, illustrations hold a vital place. Without their valuable assistance, it is difficult to achieve all four purposes.

There are various kinds of illustrations: analogies, similies, metaphors and extended metaphors, stories, parables. All of these should be used. The "I ams" of Jesus (I am the Bread of life, Water of life, Light of the world, Way, etc.) all have a wealth of meaning in the context in which they were spoken. They grow out of a rich Old Testament heritage to which they allude. Illustrative phrases, like "the lamb of God," not only illustrate truth—they do of course—but to a Jew familiar with sacrifice, they evoked memories, past teachings, and experiences, etc. When Jesus called himself the Door of the sheepfold, the entire shepherdly imagery of the Old Testament accompanied it. The connotations of the twenty-third psalm, for instance, all came alive as Jesus spoke about Himself as the good Shepherd.

So, one principle in selecting illustrations that count is to be sure that you use illustrations that elicit as much desirable response as possible from the listener. Agricultural illustrations, in a rural church (when used accurately) usually will evoke much more than in an urban church. Highly urban references will tend to have the opposite effect. Of course, the use of such references backfires when a preacher fails to gather and handle his facts with precision (just let him start talking about a "mother and father and baby bull" and see what happens in a rural congregation; but in some highly urban congregations he might even slip it by without a single member batting an eyelash!).

Yet, on the other hand, there is also an appeal that fresh, new material has when it is truly unique or unusual and when it is presented in an understandable manner. The illustrator can take nothing for granted; he must carefully describe, explain, compare, and contrast what he is talking about with what is known ("the tray, of which I am speaking, looks very much like grandma's old tin cookie sheet").

A second principle to keep in mind is that a *new use of* old, familiar, routine, or everyday material is well received. Here the threadbare, unnoticed, and droll take on a new dimension, and (in doing so) new life. Because it is commonplace, such material continues to remind the listener of the truth it illustrated during subsequent weeks, when he encounters the phenomenon. I have an illustration about a garbage can that I am sure does that. Christ words "I am the . . ." are like that; they have such an effect.

A third principle that I want to emphasize is to avoid, *at all cost*, canned, trite, worn-out illustrations, and all illustrations that come prepackaged in illustration books. Find, develop, manufacture your own. When Jesus said, "Consider the lilies of the field . . . ," doubtless He gestured toward flowers growing at His listeners' feet. With Him, you have all of God's creation as your book of illustrations; you must learn how to read it. To do so, a preacher must develop the capacity to use his senses *fully*. We have *learned* in life not to do so. We have developed the capacity to screen *out* much that goes on around us; we focus very selectively on our environment. This is necessary in growth, but it is detrimental to illustrative thinking. As a child you could be fascinated over a blade of grass on which an ant was crawling. Now, such things hardly ever capture your attention. Preachers—i.e., good preachers—have learned to become childlike once again. They open their eyes and ears to the full range of sounds and sights all about them. They taste, *and savor* whatever they eat. Their senses of touch and smell come alive again. And, from what they allow themselves to take in, they express truth as others who have lost this ability no longer can. They are keenly aware of the fact that the same God who redeemed us in Christ is the One who created the world. Therefore, there is continuity between created things and the new creation in Christ; the *whole* material world becomes fair game for illustrating spiritual truth.

How does one learn to become aware of his world so that he may use it to illustrate? He must relearn that which was natural to him as a child. I shall give you two concrete suggestions for doing so. If you follow them faithfully for six months, you will begin to experience a great change.

First, buy a small notebook that you can carry with you. Keep it for any illustrations that come your way, as it were, intruding themselves upon you. But don't just *wait* for illustrations; *seek* and you shall find! Most good illustrations are not free; they cost the preacher something.

As the first order of business every morning when you enter your study (after prayer) look around at, listen to, smell, touch what is there. Look at things you never noticed before—cracks in plaster, holes in rugs, scratches in the desk; they all contain messages if you will only read them carefully. Listen to that hum, the bird singing outside, the sound of water gurgling through a pipe in the wall. What are these sounds telling you? Nothing? Then listen, imagine, think, think, think! Run your hand over the smooth surface of the desk, the rough texture of a concrete block in the outside wall—is there a truth hidden there? Of course—at least 50 illustrations are hidden in that block alone, if only you will attune yourself to them! That pen lying on your desk, like the human beings who may use it, has potential to bless or curse others; those pages of crumpled, discarded thought in the wastebasket have a word to speak about God's attitude toward humanistic ideas; that telephone, which is your link with the outside; all these items, and thousands of others like them, are available to you for use. Focus on one—say the telephone—see how *many* different aspects of it provide illustrations. Why, the telephone alone could keep you busy manufacturing illustrations for a month!

Now, each day, write down in your notebook at least *one* illustration from your study. Don't do anything else until you do that. Don't be too concerned about how good or bad the illustration may seem. In time, you will soon discover, your illustrations will become better and better. You'll not only get the hang of discovering them more quickly, but you'll learn how to put them into words more easily. Manufacturing illustrations, before long, actually will become fun.

The second suggestion is to take your notebook into the church auditorium every week and write down at least five more illustrations from what you see or think about there. That practice will enable you during the coming weeks to point to something around you in a sermon (as Christ did in referring to the lilies) as you give an illustration ("Do you know that that chandelier over there is . . ."; "This organ that you have heard played so beautifully wouldn't work at all if. . . .").

Now, all of the illustrations above have to do with *things*. I put the emphasis on these, because they are easier to work with at first, and a preacher should *begin* with them. They are good, especially for making brief, telling points and giving sermons a touch of color and relevance here and there. But the most effective illustrations are stories and accounts of people in action ("A sower went out to sow") and/or in conversation (cf. the parable of the prodigal son). In the parables, for instance, dialog is often used with real power; it brings the listener closer to the story so that he becomes more fully involved in it. Read the parables, noting all the direct discourse that occurs (set apart by quotation marks in most modern translations), and learn!

But how can you develop stories, incidents, etc., that you may use as more extended illustrations? Basically, by (1) making up your own stories ("Suppose a farmer had just plowed his field . . ."), (2) studying good examples of story-telling wherever you can find them, and (3) keeping your eyes and ears open to what is happening around you in life wherever you are. When others are idling, with their minds in neutral, you must be looking, listening, absorbing all you can. Jot down notes immediately; otherwise, you'll forget. Then, later, work over the notes, putting the story in better form. If you follow this advice, you will find it possible to collect reams of stuff in no time. Out of it, there will be more than enough good material to use, or to revise for use.

After a minister has worked hard at this regularly, daily, he will notice something interesting beginning to happen: *as he is preaching, illustrations will pop into his head*—out of the blue. Some of these will be good; early on, most won't be so good. At first, he should wisely avoid using them on the spot as they occur. But, *as soon as the sermon is over*, he should jot them down and work them into better form later on (the major problems with them will have to do with form).

This matter of form is of importance to illustration. One must think about the best ways of wording and using an illustration. This takes time and careful thought—usually leading to the writing out of key words and phrases that you want to remember when using the illustration. That is especially true of those that depend—as many jokes do—on a "punch line" (or denouement). Sequence also can be of significance.

But for the illustration craftsman, the time will come when, after having done all these things in a disciplined way, these processes will become automatic and unconscious, so that *at last* you will be able to trust yourself to use many of those illustrations that (you will find) increasingly occur for the first time when preaching—right on the spot. They will come in proper form and sequence more and more. That is when preaching really becomes free! Then you will discover yourself writing such material into your outline *after* the sermon to use the next time you preach the sermon. But the necessary prelude to this freedom is much disciplined labor over illustrating.

Because illustrations put windows in sermons that enable people to see, you *must* use them; there are too many blind-wall sermons at which people stare blankly for half an hour or more, because they lack good illustrations. You may think that you see a truth, but do you really, until you can illustrate it? That is a pretty good test of your own understanding; and it helps preclude self-deception (which is so prevalent among us). Illustrating truth reduces fuzziness in both preacher and listener. So come alive to all of God's creation as the illustration book of spiritual truth, and then your preaching and (at length) your congregation will come alive too!

16

MORE ON "ILLUSTRATIONS"

I have never appreciated the fact that the word "illustration" is used to cover all storytelling in preaching. Because the word focuses on the *visual* alone (to illustrate is to "brighten" or "throw light on" something), it has tended to limit appeal to the other senses (hearing, smelling, tasting, touching), and that, in turn, has tended to impoverish our preaching. Perhaps it would be well if the word storytelling were to replace it altogether.

Stories, well told, are sense-oriented; they appeal to the senses. Dialog, for instance, an integral part of most good stories (see Christ's parables), appeals especially to the sense of hearing. The prodigal son talks to himself, rehearsing what he will say to his father (here, in a modern translation, you will even find quotes within quotes!—dialog with himself!).

This is an important point, about which I have said more in a chapter of a book on preaching soon to be published by Westminster Theological Seminary. But, here, I shall zero in on two issues involved in illustration (or, better, storytelling): (1) recent vs. timeless stories and (2) contrived vs. actual.

Let it be said that there are distinct advantages to each. The Bible uses all four, so I am not suggesting the elimination of one or the other but, rather, an understanding of the values of each, so that they may be selected and used more powerfully.

Recent vs. Timeless

Of course, the recent *may* become timeless, but in many instances this will not be true, and also in most cases you will not be able to make this determination beforehand. So, in choosing a given story, it is useful to remember the distinction.

Recent events, known to all (like the assassination of Anwar Sadat, president of Egypt—a contemporary and still strongly felt happening—have impact *so long as this emotional climate remains*. But the chances are, by the time that this volume can be published and distributed, and certainly in a year or so, it will have lost most (if not all) of that added impact. Such stories, then, are best used right away, but lose their impact with the passage of time (unless a great deal of background is used in order to recreate something of that feeling, so that the listener/viewer may relive the event[1]). Today, November 3, 1981, the papers are filled with the story of a Soviet submarine that ran aground in Swedish waters. Have you forgotten this story by now? Surely, even if this recalls it for you, it will be stale. So, *recent* events—widely known—are best used *right away*.

Timeless events are good any time. Certain events (Lincoln's assassination, Pearl Harbor, etc.) have that character naturally, that is, they have *become* timeless by becoming memorable over long periods of time. The preacher can refer to them and stir memories or emotions with a minimum of backfill. (Of course, any event can be used if enough background is given to recreate the event for the listener—but *that takes sermon time*—often a good bit of it.[2]) Timeless events also are reusable at any time. A sermon can be preached—stories and all—largely as it was the first time, if its examples and stories are of a timeless quality. Clearly, new materials must be sought if the stories are dated. One of the hallmarks of a *poor* reused sermon (there is nothing wrong with reusing sermons, *per se*) is stale stories.

My advice is that unless a recent event has *great* impact on the *entire* congregation, as a rule, it would be better not to use it. Moreover, if you follow the general rule, one illustration for each point, then it would be better to limit dated stories, allusions, and examples to a maximum of one per sermon. Christ seemed to use dated material sparingly, for example, "those eighteen on whom the tower in Siloam fell"; "Zecharias, son of Barachias, whom you

---

1. Clearly, the more recent the event, if it had wide impact, the less the need for a recreation of feeling in its retelling.
2. Sometimes, however, it is worth taking the time to deeply impress the truth on a congregation.

murdered between the temple and the altar." Apart from those two instances, it is difficult to find any such material.

Contrived vs. Actual

I have been discussing *actual* events thus far; not all stories, examples, etc., must be so. Christ's parables were contrived. Manufactured events ("Suppose a farmer wanted to kill the weeds in his field . . . .") have one great advantage: you can produce them and shape them precisely to the point you wish to make *at any time*. You do not need to search for them or to settle for a story that only *partially* fits. Of course, there is a disadvantage too: you must do *creative* work: some don't like to; others think they can't (on this point see my book, *Insight and Creativity in Christian Counseling*). But creative thinking, in the long run, is an advantage, because the more of it that is done, the more it tends to make one a more effective thinker and preacher. Contrived stories ought always to be presented as such—the question of their reality never should be left ambiguous.

There is also the possibility of taking an actual event and reversing it: "Suppose the Soviet submarine had been found in the San Diego harbor. . . ." Often, doing this will (1) bring an event closer to one's own sphere of activity and (2) allow for the sort of alterations that are needed to make a point from the passage being discussed.

Real stories do, however, have the value of recency, when freshly used, and (again) do not require so much time to tell. But, when one takes the time to fill in details, like many of Christ's parables, these stories become memorable.

All in all, the analysis of various options itself is what is most valuable. Think about them, be aware of what you are doing when you select a story and why you are doing so. If you take the time to do so, you will be delighted with the results.

17

IMAGINE THAT!

If you were to ask what I think is lacking in contemporary preaching, I would be hard-put to answer; there are so many failings. But, certainly, one factor that grows high on the trellis is the widespread tendency to neglect imagery.

Too much of the preaching that we hear sounds like lectures given in the chilly halls of the theological schools or, worse still, like the dusty commentaries lining the shelves of the preacher's library. Seldom do you hear preaching even remotely akin to the warm sermons of Christ, replete with parables, illustrations, examples, and figures of speech that cause them to sparkle, make them memorable, and help even the simplest listener to understand.

But it is not just in the preaching of Christ and the apostles that we find such vivid imagery; throughout history, imagery has been one of the hallmarks of great preachers—Chrysostom, Luther, Spurgeon, all made truth live by picturing it to their readers (see my book, *Sense Appeal in the Sermons of C. H. Spurgeon,* for one example of this).

But what is imagery, and how does one develop the ability to use it in preaching?

Imagery has to do with imaging, or imagining. Until a preacher can picture for himself what he is talking about, it is very doubtful that he himself adequately understands what he is trying to tell others. At any rate, it is almost certain that, apart from imagery, few, if any, of the members of his congregation will understand—even if he does.

Imagery has two dimensions: first, it is the ability to sketch the picture mentally for one's self. Then, imagery is the ability to sketch it verbally for others to see. In the fullest sense of the expression, a listener ought to be able to say after a sermon, "Ah, now I *see.*"

But how does one acquire and develop the skills that are needed to picture truth for himself and for others?

First, let me stress the importance of working harder than ever at learning how to picture truth. In biblical times, the listeners' imaginations were much more highly trained than that of today's average listener. They had to be because they had to use their imaginations so much more frequently than we do. They had no photography, no TV, no movies, no picture books, etc., to do the job for them. Instead, they themselves had to picture in their minds what they heard. Biblical writers and preachers were well aware of this and fairly freckled their messages with imagery of every kind. If in that day they recognized the necessity for imagery, how much more so is imagery in preaching needed today, when the listener's imagination is weak and flabby from disuse? In this day of untrained imaginations, we must work all the harder to assist the listener; otherwise, he will not be able to fill in the gaps for himself. Indeed, we see him bored, dozing, and wavering in the pew. He complains that the sermon was "dry." Such complaints are not altogether groundless; and at the bottom of the complaint may be the preacher's failure to picture truth.

Two factors are essential to good imagery in preaching:
1. An ability to see;
2. An ability to make others see.

This picturing the truth for one's self and for others involves a number of prerequisites, three of which have been given all too little consideration by preachers and by those who teach them. You too may have failed to notice them as they came floating by.

1. It takes time to sketch mental and verbal pictures and hound down imagery that adequately portrays a truth. Most preachers are in a hurry. They work on their sermons under pressure. They, therefore, allow too little time—if any—for putting their feet up and letting their minds wander over fields, hills, valleys, beside brooks and streams; they seldom walk mentally through cluttered city streets, stroll up dingy alleys, climb fire escapes, or peer out of the windows of a skyscraper. Their imaginations are dull and sluggish because they are so seldom given free rein to roam and romp. To do so takes time. That is the first and most important prerequisite.

2. The imagination must be exercised at other times than when looking for apt sermonic images. If it is not frequently given opportunity to range far and wide, it will not know where to go in search of those compelling pictures that are needed. Instead, when you send

it out to fetch an image for you, it will cower timidly at the front door, like a new puppy that does not feel at home in the neighborhood. One way to exercise the imagination is to read books that make demands upon it. If a preacher works with commentaries and with the sort of fare that, typically, is written for preachers all the time, and never reads anything else, he is likely to find his imaginative powers drying up quickly.

3. Prerequisite number 3 is effort. Even when the mind has had opportunity to explore and discover, the work is not complete. Proper structure, sequence, and descriptive terminology must be developed as the vehicles for conveying to others the imagery that the mind has dragged home. Otherwise, it will be bottled up in the preacher, who can't ever seem to get others to see things as he does. This is a common fault. There must be work, work roughing in each picture, giving it depth and perspective, choosing colors, refining each feature until—at last—there it hangs, finished and framed, a fair representation of what the preacher wishes to convey, in a form that makes its message immediately intelligible.

So, imagery is where it is at in preaching. Let me suggest two daily activities that, if followed regularly for a time, will get you started:

1. Every weekday, locate at least one image in the Bible. Examine it. Try to understand what it conveys to the reader and how it does so. Make a note of your results.

2. Next, think of at least one other contemporary image that might be used to portray the same truth. Try to think of a modern situation and audience with which it might be used with equal power. Again, state why you think it would do the job. Keep rereading your notes. You will notice improvement as time goes by.

Preacher, don't continue to fail your congregation because you have never understood the place and the power of imagery. Take the time to study the subject; learn all that you can about it. Do the simple exercise that I have suggested above, and start right away. If you do, I can almost guarantee that in time you will begin to receive compliments on your sermons—imagine that!

18

MAKE YOUR PREACHING LIVE

"How can I make my preaching come alive and bring a passage home to my congregation in a vivid and memorable way?" Hundreds of times every year this question, together with a score of related ones, is asked by seminary students, pastors, and—in reverse form—long-suffering members of congregations. What is the answer?

There is no *"the* answer." Answering that question is a complex matter—far more complex than the *partial* answer that I shall attempt to spell out here. And—to make matters worse—style (which is a significant factor in the total answer) is so individualized that the answer is not the same for everybody. John the Baptist and Christ came preaching with very different styles (Matt. 11:16-19), yet both were extremely effective communicators.

So, what I am interested in here is a *beginning* in which *some* of the more universally applicable principles of good preaching may be discussed. Obviously, many other matters—both general and particular—could be mentioned in addition to or instead of these. However, as a former teacher of homiletics (and speech) for 17 consecutive years, I can assure you that work on the matters that I am now raising will go a long way toward improvement. They all have to do with form.

But first, let me commend you (if you have continued to read this far) for your concern. You can be sure that there are many preachers—content with what they have been doing—who have put down the book already. In many cases (of course) they are the ones who need it most. Hundreds of congregations put up with dull, lifeless, uninteresting preaching of the most interesting and vital subject matter in the world. More to the point—young and old alike are turned away from or (at least) turned off to Christianity by preaching that unwittingly misrepresents God's truth by the distortions that take place as the result of the communicator's deadness. Much of this is due to an inexcusable laxity with which so many Bible-believing pastors proclaim God's vibrant truth. I am not excusing congregations for allowing themselves to be turned off, or for not doing something to rectify this deplorable situation. That is their fault. Many members for years put up with the sort of stuff they wouldn't accept even from a TV news reporter—and they *know* it is bad. Their children are adversely affected, they wouldn't dare bring an unsaved person with them to church, etc. But they do nothing about it—except, perhaps, gripe among themselves. It would be better to confront the pastor himself (lovingly) and see what could be done. They don't; so everyone suffers. *That*, I say, is their fault. And they must bear their share of responsibility for accepting such fare. But the poor preaching itself isn't their fault. It is yours, pastor, and you must do something about it if you stand condemned by these words.

Now, I said I wanted to commend you. Does it sound like I have ended up by condemning you instead? Sorry, that wasn't my intention. You are on the right track if you are prayerfully concerned and working at the problem. Stick to it, and in time things will get better. So, pastor, on behalf of your congregation, let me thank you for taking the time to consider a subject like this! Now, to the matters at hand.

Actually I have been talking about the matter already. It is this: take the time and make the effort to *work on form*. Too many preachers think that if they spend all of their time in the supermarket selecting food for the family meal, they have done enough. They will be quick to tell you, "After all, good exegesis costs something. I have paid high prices to select the very best, purest products. Exegesis is the real thing. What counts is faithfulness to the text—understanding and interpreting it plainly. If I do that successfully, why should I have to bother with form? Shouldn't the congregation get excited over truth—*God's truth*—regardless of form?"

So they reason; and (I'll grant you) at first it sounds convincing. It is *very* convincing to those who have good reasons for wanting to rationalize about the matter. But when you think it through there is a reason for focusing on form. "What is it? Why shouldn't my congregation be satisfied—indeed *pleased*—with the food I deliver every week?" I'll tell you why—because they can't eat raw potatoes! That's why!

Think it through a bit. You are asking, "Why can't the family be excited if my wife returned home with shopping bags loaded with the finest foods available? Why should they complain if she said, 'Food selection is everything; don't ask me to prepare, cook, and serve it too. You should appreciate this food because it is good. You need it. It constitutes a well-balanced meal, etc.' " How would you like it if for supper tonight she put a bag on the table and told you to have a go at it. There was the cauliflower still in a wrapper, a box of uncooked rice, a couple of raw slabs of filet mignon, unground coffee beans in your cup, and a box of do-it-yourself Betty Crocker chocolate cake? Would you be turned on by that? Would you grow—even if the meal was well balanced and nourishing?

The analogy is not altogether inappropriate. Many pastors spend little or no time beyond exegesis preparing to make truth edible. Consequently, God's hungry family goes away unfed. The pastor wonders why they don't grow: "The food was there, but they didn't eat; why?" It is not enough to protest, "If they are hungry, let them eat!" What are they going to do with that uncooked rice and those coffee beans? No matter how nutritious the ingredients of a meal may be, little eating will take place where it is not properly prepared. You are the cook; serve God's truth in a savory, appetizing way—man does not live by bread alone!

It sounds very pious to talk about spending all your time on exegesis and interpretation. But let me make it very clear that form and content are really inseparable. Just as the true flavors of the meats and vegetables cannot be appreciated until they are properly cooked, so too there can be no adequate understanding or appreciation of many biblical truths until they are put in a form that is compelling to the listener.

Form does not clothe truth—as some have erroneously taught (that's like dousing a filet mignon with ketchup and mustard until you can't taste the meat)—no, it brings out the natural flavor of the truth itself.

And, let it be noted, *there will be form*—of one kind or another—whenever God's truth is preached; form is unavoidable. But wrapped cauliflower on the plate and beans in the coffee cup are *bad form for eating!* Such form actually *distorts.* Coffee is to be drunk, not chewed! If the interpreter fails to prepare the meal in such a way that he brings out all the flavors of truth inherent in the passage, using them for the purposes intended by the Holy Spirit under whose moving power they were inerrantly written, he may understand the passage himself (though this is doubtful), but he certainly does not faithfully interpret it to the congregation. Make no mistake about it; bad form can ruin good content.[1]

All right! If form means so much, how does one go about improving form? The suggestions that follow may be helpful. None is worked out fully, but presented only suggestively. Further chapters could be written on each (and hopefully, in time, will be). Here they are, briefly presented:

1. *Wash out all "preachy" language and "syntax."*

The rule here is to use no unnecessary special words or expressions. An example is the word *beloved*. We simply don't use that word in public address today. *Friends* usually is an excellent substitute (incidentally, you can't really "wash out" such language; rather you must *replace* it. Until, by practice, you have developed a new, better way of saying something—and it has become habitual to you to do so—don't deceive yourself into thinking you have eliminated the problem).

By syntax I mean especially the archaisms (coming from the AV sentence structure) of 1611 that in English persist only in the pulpit. Constructions like "the person of Christ" should be replaced with contemporary ones such as "Christ's person." (That is, if the word "person" is integral to what you want to say; frequently, it is added for no purpose when it would be better simply to say "Christ": e.g., "Believe in Christ as your Savior," not, "Believe in the person of Christ as your Savior.") The use of "for" in those constructions in which it introduces a reason (e.g., "for he did not know that . . .") should be replaced by "since" or "because" or often by a semicolon.

2. *Replace or explain all technical terms.*

Words like sanctification, justification, salvation are important and

---

[1]. Of course, God can (and obviously does) still use His Word in spite of form. But it is not the interpreter's right to distort and misrepresent content by inappropriate form.

must not be eliminated from preaching. Since they can't, they *must* be explained. Explanation need not always be direct ("sanctification means . . ."), but more often may be more indirect (". . . results in sanctification, that growth in grace by which one puts off old sinful practices and replaces them with new righteous ones. . . .").

All technical terms not necessary for preaching (though they may be essential for seminary education) should be avoided altogether. Thus "eschatology" usually can be avoided by referring to the Bible's teachings about the future. Longer? Of course; that's one reason we use technical terms. But are technical terms *clearer?* No; not unless one understands the term precisely.

How does one come to recognize the prevalence of preachy and technical language? The easiest way is to (1) Tape your sermons over a period of time and make careful notations. (2) Develop, write out, and frequently refer to alternatives with which to replace poor terms, and begin to use them. In time, the tape recorder should reveal whether the transition and substitution has taken place. (3) Each preacher can make a growing list of the problems he notes in others and check these over against his own preaching. In such ways—by taking the time and effort—many men have radically transformed their preaching form in less than six months.

3. *Check the accuracy, precision, and appropriateness of the words you use.*

Again, use the tape recorder. But this time you are looking for abstract, general, overworked, and vague words. *Things* is a typical example that combines all of the qualities of hazy, dull, uninformative speech. Whenever a specific term can be used, do so. Instead of using the word *thing,* say what it is that this word blocks from view. Also look for words like *car.* To speak of "a black '78 Vet" says a lot more and conjures up an image in the listener's mind. Say "car," and he may erroneously picture a bright red cadillac. It takes more effort and time and thought to be exact, but the rewards are great. Use of the dictionary, and especially *Roget's Thesaurus* (best in dictionary form[2]) should become a habit. Reading good material—and analyz-

---

2. This book, together with Rudolf Flesch's *The ABC of Style,* always should be at hand, and well used.

ing what makes it good—is another habit to form. Life and vividness come through precision and accuracy in word choice.

4. *Use good illustrative material.*

Spurgeon has written the classic work on illustration in his *Art of Illustration*. I don't need to repeat what he has said there. While I certainly don't recommend all of Donald Gray Barnhouse's teachings, I surely urge you to read all of his works, in order to learn how to use illustrations. He could make a truth, or an error, *live*.

Illustrative materials are of two sorts (when viewed from one perspective): short examples and longer incidents. Jesus used common everyday items around Him (bread, water, doors, sheep) for shorter illustrations. Then, He told parables. Here, there were usually people in action and often in conversation (even when unlikely: the rich fool talks to himself; so does the prodigal son who—believe it or not—quotes himself to himself; check it out!). I suggest that many of your illustrations become stories in which you use direct discourse. Get rid of the reporter's third person. Begin by determining to enter into a book at least one illustration of each sort each day for six months. In time you'll see the improvement.

I have given four suggestions. Obviously these are but a beginning, as I said before. But they are a good place to begin, and should occupy a man who is serious about it for at least six months.

19

PREACHING RHYTHMS

One of the principal unrecognized problems in contemporary preaching is sleep-inducing rhythm patterns. These pulpit lullabies, which stroke and soothe already sleepy parishioners, are of much more frequent occurrence and contribute far more toward the ineffectiveness of preaching than most realize.

Pulpit sirens, who fall into such rhythmic patterns, can bill and coo at congregations unwittingly. It is almost impossible to convince them that their Sunday lyrics may be responsible for the small results obtained, because of the difficulty of recognizing the problem in one's own preaching. If you are guilty of orchestrating weekly performances of this nature, you will never know it unless you are willing to listen analytically to tapes of your preaching in a critical and businesslike manner. Because so few are, I predict that this article will go largely unheeded. Pastoral nightingales, perched in pulpits, chirruping and warbling away, often are too entranced with the sound of their own voices to do the critical evaluation necessary. But for the few rare birds who will listen, who discover that the problem is theirs and who wish to do something about it, I offer the following suggestions.

I. *Recognize What Your Pattern Is*

While these preaching rhapsodies differ according to the pulpit musician, there are four major variables that appear in all patterns. They are:

1. Sentences of relatively the same length.
2. Repetition of standardized pitch patterns.
3. Repetition of standardized accent (or beat) patterns.
4. Pattern in control of content rather than growing out of content.

Sentences of the same length form the basis for sing-song and other melody patterns. The only way to break this habit is to consciously replace it with both sentences that are chopped off and sentences that are extended. Verbal exclamation points and semicolons would help.

Repetition of standardized pitch patterns, combined with sentences of similar length, produce a sing-song tune as well as other lilting airs that may be attractive enough at points but begin to cuddle, coddle, and caress when in regular profusion. Beginning or ending sentences on the same pitch level, rising to heights at the end or trailing off into plains after descending from the heights, when used over and over, sentence after sentence, may sound mellow and poetic but do not grip.

Repetition of standardized accent patterns add a jerky monotonous element that sounds like bad poetry: da da ´ da da ´ da da ´ da da ´, da da ´ da da ´ da da ´; da da ´ da da ´ da da ´ da da ´, da da ´ da da ´ da da ´. Break them up. Working on varying the length of your sentences will have a salutary effect; you cannot slide into the pattern unless the length of sentences allows it. This problem, then, is a complication of the first problem and dependent on it.

Pattern in control of content. Content, at all points, should control whatever else takes place in a sermon. Not all patterns are wrong, but one pattern throughout always is. Patterns, when appropriate, appear and disappear. They shift with content. An obvious example is the pattern that I have named *question clusters.* In great preaching, at emotional heights in the sermon, there often appear a cluster of questions—one after another. This pattern can be very effective, if not overdone and if it is used appropriately. But to use this pattern where there is *no height to which to rise,* or to use it again and again, is to destroy a good thing. Much more might be said about every one of these elements, but my concern here is to identify them, not to discuss them in depth.

II. *Practice Alternative Patterns*

Until you identify (from sermon tapes) exactly what patterns (or combinations of the four factors mentioned above) happen to be yours, you can do nothing about them. But assuming that you have isolated one or two patterns (we tend to have several and overwork one or the other for a while), you are now ready to do something about them. On the basis of the biblical put off/put on principle,[1] you must

---

1. See *The Christian Counselor's Manual* for more on this.

recognize that it is not enough to attempt to "break" (put off) a habit; you must *replace* it with its biblical alternative.

Notice that in elements 1 to 3 meaningless *repetition*[2] is the basic problem. Repetitive length, repetitive pitch patterns, and a repetitive cadence are the culprits that we have been uncovering. Therefore, the alternative is *variety:* variety in sentence length, in pitch patterns, and in accent patterns. How can it best be effected?

Variety must not be used merely for variety's sake. Largely, variety will come when content controls speech patterns. This is true because as content varies, patterns that grow out of content and seek to serve it will follow. The content and its mood itself, if carefully followed, will bring about variety.

The problem, then, is to practice (outside of actual preaching contexts) wedding melody and rhythm patterns to content. Exciting content usually calls for extremes in length—staccato sentences or lengthy, periodic ones. More measured, relaxed, background or other factual materials call for more moderated lengths (though there is to be variety in this too). Pitch tends to rise with strong emotion, and drops with less emotional content. There will be a lot more high notes in the former and fewer in the latter.

Knowing what factors to work with will make the difference. However, don't think you can make the change all at once. Have patience. Work, regularly, for six weeks or more (every day), and you will discover the new patterns beginning to take hold. So will your congregation.

---

2. Repetition, properly used, can be meaningful, helpful, and powerful.

20

DOES THIS APPLY TO YOU?

In seminary, in one form or another, you were taught "Be sure to apply the truth that you are teaching." That is good advice; it follows biblical precedent and precept and points to an important fact that continually needs to be reemphasized. But *how* does one apply truth to life? On that question advice differs and/or often thins out. It is easy to gain assent to various truisms and noble goals, but it is when you turn to the discussion of ways and means that differences begin to appear. Everyone wants peace. So far, agreement is easy, but people will battle fiercely over how to obtain it. So too, all homileticians insist on the necessity for application but argue for widely differing methods of applying truth. Therefore, I shall focus my comments not so much on the commonplace areas of agreement but on the points of difference, in an attempt to provide some sort of guidelines for proceeding through this homiletic maze.

I

To begin with, briefly let us consider the meaning of the word "application," so that we may understand from the outset what it is that we are discussing. The verb *apply* etymologically means "to fold or lay upon." The idea of "attachment" is also connected with it, but, as one word book puts it, to apply means "to attach firmly so it will not come off." That idea is clearly seen in the use of the word in the following sentence: "He applied a coat of paint to the door." The paint is firmly bonded to the door. So in sermonic application, something is laid upon or attached to the truth that is being taught. That means that application
1. is a step beyond mere teaching (thought of as the communication of factual knowledge), and
2. requires something more of the preacher than an understanding or proper interpretation of a preaching portion.

What application does, then, is to "attach" to the simple interpretation of the passage the meaning for the congregation today in the context of their modern life situations. *Folded* into or *laid* upon the passage as originally understood by those who first read it is another layer of interpreted information about the congregation growing out of the present circumstances in which they find themselves.

But what this means is that not only must the preacher study the passage for its historical/grammatical meanings, but he also must
1. study the present situation (or situations) that the congregation faces,
2. study the various members of the congregation who are facing it,
3. abstract the truth or principle that the Holy Spirit intended to teach from the passage,
4. discover how the writer applied this principle to his readers, and
5. do the same today for his own congregation in their modern setting.

So, application requires something other than *using* (or, perhaps more appropriately we should say *mis*using) a preaching portion for one's own purposes. Rather, it involves discovering
1. the Holy Spirit's *telos* (or purpose) and
2. *how the Spirit directed the biblical writers to apply truth* in their day.

Sometimes, the situations in Old Testament Israel as in Corinth (or in both) will be exactly the same as they are today—death, for instance, is death, no matter where or when one faces it. It is not conditioned by time or culture. The application of I Corinthians 15:54-58, then, will be found, and may be used substantially as it is found, in the passage itself.

But veils, as a sign of the husband's authority over his wife, are another matter altogether; they simply do not have that meaning in modern Western culture. Consequently, while the principle of order and decorum in worship that pertains to a woman's submission to her husband must still be applied, it will be possible to do so only if we attach or fold in a layer of new material that fits the present situation.

II

But now we come to the *how to*. What is involved in attaching, folding in, or unfolding the biblically attached applicatory layer of a sermon? As I said, this is where differences appear and the arguments begin.

Calvin and the early Reformers show by their sermons and commentaries that they held to a view of the matter that is at great variance with the approach followed by so many preachers and homileticians today. Perhaps that is why (in part at least) modern preaching has so much less impact than theirs did. What happened to change the course of Protestant preaching?

The scholastic views of the Middle Ages that Luther and Calvin abandoned were later reintroduced into preaching in Protestant circles by a number of the English Puritans who had never shaken loose of them. As a result, their commentaries and the examples that their sermons set turned back the clock on effective preaching for several generations. Because their approach to application (which they believed in with a vengeance) still constitutes the prevailing model (in a greatly revised form), we are yet strongly under their influence. These two approaches to application—what I may roughly call the Reformation approach and the Puritan approach—readily set forth for us the choice that one must make in preaching. And, as you have already gathered from the tenor of the discussion so far, I take my stand with the Reformers against what I hold to be the corrupting influence of the Puritans. How did the two differ?

For the Reformers, the whole sermon was application; what was added, attached, or folded in was done naturally, organically, as an integral part of the whole. From start to finish, as they interpreted the Scriptures for the congregation, *at the same time,* they preached what the text had to say about the people sitting before them. Application was made all along.

In contrast, the Puritans exposited the text (often that is not the right way to put it either—many of them had a penchant for doing anything but exposition. Instead, they often taught a systematic theology lesson on words that triggered their interest, at times quite heedless of the Holy Spirit's intentions in the particular passage at hand); then they tacked on at the end of the sermon various and sundry "uses" or "improvements on the text" by way of application. Again, most of their applications had little to do with the point made by the Spirit in the passage which, by this time, had become a springboard for whatever they wished to say. While in modern times the number of applicatory "uses" has been greatly reduced, so that, fortunately, we rarely hear of thirteenthlies or fourteenthlies any more, unfortunately the idea of tacking on the application at the end has persisted.

Instead, we must learn to proclaim and apply the entire preaching portion throughout the sermon—even in the exposition—as the Reformers did, namely, as God's Word to the congregation. Instead of saying throughout the sermon, "This is what God said to the Israelites," and then, at the very end, asking, "Now what does all this mean to us today?" the preacher from the outset ought to tell his people, "This is what God says to *you*. How do we know this? Well, listen to what he told the Israelites, who were facing circumstances not altogether unlike your own. . . ." There is just as much exposition in the one approach as in the other; the great difference lies in the fact that the Reformation approach is relevant, up-to-date, and treats the Word of God as a message to people today, while the other does not.

The Puritan approach lets the congregation dangle throughout the greater part of the sermon. They wonder what the preacher is up to, what is the point of all this exposition. And if at length they become interested in facts for facts' sake alone, it is understandable. Only at the end does one discover what the preacher has in mind when the application is finally made (if it is; some have taken the next logical step and eliminated it altogether). And at the end it is so easy to make applications that have little to do with the passage since by then it has been left behind. N.B., it is harder to depart from the Holy Spirit's applicatory purpose when you are making application as a part of the exposition itself. How much better, then, if in the introduction the preacher orients the congregation to look for personal applications throughout as he investigates the meaning of the passage with them. This orientation may take several forms. I shall note two:

1. *The solution to a problem* (or answer to a question).

"Have you wondered what God has to say about the discipline of children in your home (note well, *not* what He had to say to the Israelites)? Well, let's turn to Proverbs 29:15 and to Ephesians 6:4 and see." Notice how the listener is personally involved from the start. When the text is considered, it is considered as God's Word to *him;* not merely to someone else long ago and far away. All that is discovered in the passage is easily related immediately—when the listener still remembers it—to *him:* "So, it is clear that God wants you to use not only the rod but also reproof; not only discipline but also counsel. If you fail to emphasize both in balance, God says that you will run the risk of provoking your children to anger." That is the way to apply biblical truth; that is the way to *preach!*

2. *Exhortation to obey a command.*

"God commands you to love your wife. In Ephesians 5 He says...." Here, once again, the listener becomes involved directly in the teaching of the Scriptures from the beginning. The passage is treated for what it is in truth—the Word of God for *him.*

What I have said elsewhere about outlines also is appropriate here. In order to impress on the preacher as well as on the congregation the present relevance of the passage, it is well to "translate" long-ago-and-far-away outlines into here-and-now ones. Consider the following with its "translations":

Basic modern Puritan-type outline

I. Paul told the Ephesian husbands to love their wives.
II. They were to love their wive as Christ loved the church.
III. They were to be willing to give up their lives for them.
IV. Husbands today must also love their wives.

The above "translated" into a
Basic modern Reformer-type outline

I. God commands you to love your wife.
II. You must love her as Christ loved the church.
III. You must be willing to give your life for her.

Note, there is no point IV in the Reformer-type outline because the structure of the sermon framed around the meaning and application of the text to the congregation precludes it; the sermon throughout is application.

If what you have read here applies to you, then apply it. Learn to preach the entire sermon to the congregation, dealing from start to finish with their relationship to God and to their neighbors. You will soon begin to see the good effects of this change.

21

PREACHING WITH PERSONALIZED HOW-TO

I have become increasingly concerned about the poor quality of preaching that I hear today. I am convinced that the streams flowing into this muddy river are numerous (and varied), and in the essays in this book I have been trying to row our way up a number of them in order to discover the sources of the pollution.

Elsewhere I have already spoken about the problems of form and content,[1] but I have said all too little about a kindred matter: the important place of application (or, better, *personalized how-to*) in the sermon. Let me try to correct that deficiency here and now by setting forth something helpful in this area.

The average conscientious conservative preacher (I say this from years of close observation and study) spends 95 to 100 percent of his time on content—mastering the historical and grammatical aspects of his passage. His concern is exegesis, though he more often than not lacks concern for the *telic* note in this study (see other essays on this). While I have no desire to see him do less exegetical work (indeed, any number need to do *much more*), I believe he must not stop there (I have discussed ways and means of finding time in an earlier essay). In fact, in my opinion, exegetical work forms but half of his task in preparing a message. The other half ought to be divided equally between the development of form (that fits the content, the occasion, and the congregation) and applicatory, personal, how-to materials that give direction to doctrine and help the listener put feet on facts.

It is about that last quarter of the task that I wish to speak.

When one thinks of *application* alone, he may think of colorful illustrations of biblical truth, examples of the point being made—all calculated to show *that* the issue has relevance to the congregation

1. See especially my monograph, *Communicating with Twentieth Century Man*.

addressed. So far, so good. That is necessary since, as Paul's comments in I Corinthians 10:6, 11 and 9:9, 10 indicate, there are many who must have this fact spelled large for them. But, for most, so far as application goes, that's just about as far as application goes. That is why I have spoken not so much of application as of personalized how-to.

The word *personalized* means what I have just referred to in the previous paragraph—the truncated view of application that has as its concern making clear that what the passage says has to do with (1) people today and (2) the very people who are being addressed. To do this adequately, one must learn something of audience analysis, but I shall say more about that in another essay. (The principles used are similar in a number of respects to the principles of data gathering used in counseling; for more on that, see my book, *The Christian Counselor's Manual*.)

The other side of the phrase that I have used to describe a fuller notion of application is *how-to*.

In any number of places I have mentioned the need for how-to help in counseling, but I have said very little about how-to in preaching. But how-to in preaching is needed no less than in counseling.

In my book, *Update on Christian Counseling,* Volume 1 (pp. 24-31), I have examined the Sermon on the Mount rather extensively, demonstrating that Jesus used how-to in His preaching. I shall not duplicate that work here, but I may say (by way of summary) that the inescapable conclusion I reached was that Jesus *makes no point to which He does not append how-to help* (often including as well how *not* to exhortations, directions, and examples).

What do I mean by *how-to help?* Let me just quote briefly a word or two from my study in *Update:*

> "But what happens when, in this world of sin, they do allow such things to come between them?" someone might ask. Jesus anticipates the situation, and (in very practical *how-to*—here even step-by-step—terms) He tells us *how* to handle the situation (Matt. 5:23, 24). The practical how-to comes in the form of a procedure growing out of the priority of reconciliation (p. 27).

And,

> In verses 43-48, Jesus continues this basic theme: a Christian

must *love* his enemies. But, unlike many modern preachers, Christ didn't leave the concept of love hanging in thin air—undefined and amorphous. Rather, He was quite specific: love focuses on the other person; not on one's self. Therefore (note the specific how-to) a Christian must pray for his enemies. That concrete proposal Paul developed (as we must develop all such suggestions) in Romans 12:14ff. (p. 28).

When He condemns praying as the Gentiles and hypocrites do, He not only describes plainly the forbidden practices that He has in mind, but in each instance (as well) tells us what the *proper practice in prayer* is; in other words, He tells us not only *how not to pray*, but also *how to pray*. As a matter of fact, the well-known Lord's prayer was given as an instance of such how-to help.

Many people in the pews are discouraged because they know a lot of *what-to* from the Bible, but they have never been given any *how to* help; and so they fail. When they fail again and again and again, they become deeply discouraged; some begin to doubt their salvation or God's power, while others settle back into mediocrity, saying, "Well, Paul may be able to do it, but I'm not Paul." I have seen many such lethargic Christians come alive again when given some how-to.

Well, then, how to do how-to, that is the next question to consider.

How-to is avoided because it takes work and much thought on the part of the preacher. It demands the exercise of a degree of creativity also.[2] Preachers, pressured by demands and pressed for time (even when aware of the need), characteristically omit such work. But to do so is to threaten the value of all the exegesis that one has done. It is cruel to demand of congregations what they are never taught *how* to perform. Much of the congregation whipping that goes on in Bible-believing pulpits stems directly from the frustration of pastors who think that exhortation and beatings are necessary when what is really needed is simple how-to instruction.

According to Titus 1:1, truth is designed to lead to godliness; it is not simply to be filed away in the memories of the members of the congregation for quick retrieval at the next Sunday school Bible quiz! Truth must be transformed into *life* and *ministry*. But that takes *how-to*.

2. For more on creativity, see my book, *Insight and Creativity*.

There are a few persons in a congregation who know *how-to* turn abstract material into personalized *how-to* for themselves on their own. But most don't; so the first point is that, like Christ, *the preacher must suggest ways and means of implementing every truth that he teaches.*

Where does he get such material? From looking at how he himself implements the truth in his own life (perhaps one reason for the failure in preaching is our own failure to practice what we ought to preach). He also learns from observing how other growing Christians have done so and from just plain sitting and prayerfully sweating out new ideas about ways and means.[3] I, myself, work best with pen and paper. Even when I have only the merest glimmerings of an idea, I begin to write. After a lot of scribbling over one page, throwing away another, and weighing what I have written on 8 or 10 pages over against one another, invariably I come up with a couple of viable suggestions. But usually, apart from such effort—zilch! The most important point at the outset is to get started.

The second point is that how-to material always must grow out of biblical principles and be appropriate to them *in every detail*. The end *never* justifies the means (not even in small details); the Bible alone can do so.

Thirdly, it is wise to give at least a *couple* of suggestions when offering possible how-to help because (1) we must make it clear that such suggestions (unlike the biblical commands which they seek to implement) are not inspired (God has *commanded* us to read the Bible; but while beginning with the Gospel of John *may be a wise plan in some cases*, it has no such biblical authority); (2) one suggested plan for implementing a biblical principle may appeal to or fit one person and his situation, whereas it may not fit another quite so well.

More could be said, but I'd go wrong to end without giving you a how-to suggestion, so here it is. In order to get into the (good) habit of thinking in terms of how-to, why not mimeograph a batch of 8½" x 11" worksheets for use in sermon preparation? On these sheets

---

3. I am, of course, speaking of preaching from those passages in which, unlike the Sermon on the Mount, the Bible itself give no hints about how-to. (How-to is closely related to teaching in preaching and counseling.)

(mostly consisting of blank yellow space[4]) add, among other things that you want to remember to do (e.g., "What is the *telos* of this passage?"[5]), this question, "What how-to help may be given for implementing each command?"

You say, "But you suggested giving at least a second idea—have you got one?" Of course, I could give many. But here's one more. When you've arrived at the *telos* (the Holy Spirit's purpose in giving the preaching portion—and therefore yours; i.e., what He *intends* to do to the listener through that passage), tell it to your wife. If you aren't clear about this, she'll tell you so (and you will need to get it clear before you can work on implementation). But if you are clear enough, tell her always to ask you: "But how would you suggest that I begin to do this?"

Best wishes to you, your wife, and your congregation!

---

4. More motivational than white pages.
5. See essays on telic preaching (i.e., preaching with purpose).

22

BODILY ACTION IN PREACHING

Where does one begin when he attempts to discuss this vitally important matter? "How important is it, anyway?" you may ask. More important than some of you who give no attention to it may think. "Well, why do you say that? How can you know it is important?" Because—and this is fundamental—bodily action either assists in the communication of God's message, or it hinders; there is no third ground.

How may it hinder? A lively, important biblical theme (for instance), ground through the grid of a lifeless body, can quickly lose its sense of urgency and importance. If the preacher is unwilling to allow God's truth to affect him as it ought, he will *always* communicate *something different from* that which was intended in the portion of Scripture from which he is preaching. That is the crucial point. I am not interested in oratory for the sake of oratory. The oratorical movement of a generation or two ago was way off base. Preachers, caught up in it, became more concerned about *sermons* than about preaching (there is a significant difference). Oratorical tricks and skills were intended to enhance the sermon, which was viewed as a work of art. All such thinking is as unbiblical as studying the Bible for its literary beauty alone.

No, the reason I am concerned about bodily action is not because I wish to exalt either the preacher or his sermon; my concern in this matter is to exalt Jesus Christ! My purpose is partly negative, therefore: lack of attention to proper bodily action will distort God's Word. It is also positive: good bodily action will assist in faithfully proclaiming God's truth. Let us examine, briefly, some ways in which this is so.

I

To begin with, let me lay down the fundamental guideline concerning all bodily action in preaching:

Bodily action, at every point, must grow out of and be entirely appropriate to the content of the Bible that one is proclaiming.

Keep this rule in mind. Develop your bodily action from it, and you will not go very far wrong.

Some persons preach every subject the same way. There is, for example, the perennial grinner or smiler. Somewhere, at some time, someone (perhaps his mom or dad) told him that if he continually smiled when preaching, he would have a pleasing and pleasant appearance in the pulpit. Now, there are times to smile, of course; perhaps many of us should smile much more than we do. But the fellow I have in mind has so cultivated the habit of smiling (or grinning), that even when he is preaching about hell, suffering, affliction, pain—or any one of a score of other such subjects—he continues to smile throughout. That smile, connected to any such subject, appears to listeners to be more of a sadistic leer than "pleasing and pleasant." And not only does it turn off listeners, but it grossly distorts the underlying emotional tones of warning, grief, concern, or compassion that pervade the passages from which he is preaching. What he does is almost like removing a pickle from the liquid in the jar, washing it completely free of brine and spices, then pouring Karo syrup over it in profusion. The two do not mix well.

The illustration about the smile is, of course, exaggerated, and probably exceptional (but it does exist—I have known a number of smilers and grinners). The opposite extreme—the sourpuss preacher who always either scowls, whines, cries, or looks grave and somber—may be an even more frequent offender. Naturally, there are times to be stern in preaching (when the text is), and there are times to be solemn (ditto to the previous parenthesis), but there also are times *not* to be. How can the *good news* of the gospel be proclaimed properly by a face that declares to all who behold it that the world probably will end in doom in fifteen minutes? How can *God's love* be preached effectively, without great loss, by one who whines about it? How can the zeal and enthusiasm that burst from any number of scriptural preaching portions be rightly conveyed by one who douses everything he says with his funereal manner? No, bodily action is not unimportant, because what a preacher does may speak so loudly that his congregation cannot hear what God says.

Don't think that the emotional overtones and undertones are not important. (These are conveyed equally by the voice and by bodily action.) Doubtless, a number of persons have been turned away from the truth by the pompous-sounding tones and stiff-as-a-board actions of many a preacher. This ministerial tone (or tune, or drone, as it is variously called) doubtless arises from an attempt to add a note of authority and solemnity to preaching. Because those who develop it tend to blanket all their speech with it (even announcing the young people's hot dog roast with solemn, sonorous, authoritative dignity), they make the ministry a mockery and drive those very same young people out of the church.

Stiff-as-a-board bodies and expressionless faces won't solve the problem, either. One cannot dodge the issue by trying to remain neutral or unaffected. God's truth cannot be proclaimed with objectivity or without commitment. Involved commitment almost always shows through, as, indeed, it should. Read the Scriptures—pathos, joy, concern, grief—all these tones and more protrude. The biblical writers didn't hide their feelings when writing; their writings are not like a bloodless Ph.D. thesis. Their involvement is felt throughout. Can you imagine them *preaching* with any less involvement, then? Preaching is generally much more animated and less subdued than writing.

II

"What, then, can be done?" you ask. You may have bad habits of bodily expression that distort God's message; I may have been speaking directly to you. But it is not enough to leave you there. Something must be done to effect a change. Let me suggest how that change may be brought about.

I. *Isolate the problem and in writing spell it out in detail.* Together with your wife and/or trusted persons, view and listen to your preach-

ing with the idea of discovering precisely *what* bodily factors distract (by calling attention to themselves rather than to the message) and distort (by cramming a message into a mold which it doesn't fit). Spell these out on paper. For example:
1. "Don't use hands enough, even when subject manner is animated!"
2. "Gestures are wooden, awkward; not smooth."
3. "Gestures are ill-timed; come late."
4. "Gestures are artificial."
5. "Gesture only with hands; don't use head, whole body."
6. "Smile too little."
7. "Look stiff; no movement."
8. "Move too much—movement distracting—swaying."
9. "No eye contact."
10. "Never point at congregation" (ask yourself, do you ever say "you"?).

II. *Determine what you ought to be doing instead.* With help from others, books (see my *Pulpit Speech*), write out the first step in your Personal Improvement Program; e.g.:
1. "Must learn to use hands to *describe* ('it was this tall'), *indicate* ('over *there*'), *emphasize* ('Never!')."
2. "Must synchronize gestures with speech."

III. *Determine how to make improvements.* Write out the rest of your P.I.P.
1. Every day (regularity is important), Monday through Saturday (not when preaching) I will work on using my hands in three ways.
2. At lunch (tack it to something that occurs regularly) I will tell a story, describe something, etc., that calls for the use of animated gestures, and when doing so, I'll practice.
3. Monday through Friday, when I come home, I'll describe to my wife, with gestures, something that happened that day.
4. Every night, I'll tell my children a bedtime story with grossly exaggerated gestures. Here, especially, I'll try out new ones, along with noises, facial expressions, etc. They'll love it; hopefully I'll improve.

5. I will allow the results of these exercises to bleed over into my preaching.

I can guarantee you, if you are willing to do so *regularly*, within six weeks you (and others) will notice a marked difference. If you don't believe me (and if there is no other problem—fear of embarrassment, for instance[1]), try it, and see.

---

[1] On this, see *Pulpit Speech*, pp. 154ff.

23

A STUDY OF TAPED SERMONS

The best way to study sermons is through video tape, where the full impact of delivery (the use of voice *and body*) as well as content comes through. But we are only on the edge of such capability on a widespread scale. So for the present we must be contented with what we have: audio tapes. Yet, we can learn much from them if we use them wisely. But before we learn to use them, we must learn to choose them.

Audio tapes now provide a large source, readily available. And, to use these tapes properly is of great help. But the problem is, there are *so many tapes*. How does a preacher determine which ones are worth studying? The main point of this essay is to give you guidelines for selection.

Obviously, bodily action will be absent, and something of the sermon will be lost, but in choosing tapes to study you must make allowance for that fact. (To discover how much is conveyed by the body, turn off the TV sound and watch the picture alone. Note how much bodily action occurs; discover the important use of facial expression to disclose many emotional nuances. Watch, especially, the use of hands and the tilt and movement of the body.[1])

Initial Selection

When using audio tapes, listen first for total impact—don't try to analyze the sermon yet (to analyze something is to separate out its various elements); that may come next. If you are not impressed by it, don't waste further time on it. Put it aside at once. If, on the basis of total impact, you believe the sermon is worthy of more careful study

---

1. Clearly, this will convince you that (unless the sermon is made for listening only) significant elements will be missing.

(and those that are seem to be few and far between these days), then in order to determine whether the message is worth keeping as a model to study further, I suggest the following method of analysis:[2]

I. *Verbal Analysis*

Play (and re-play) the sermon for verbal (auditory) analysis. What do you hear? (I am not thinking here of content.) Is the pitch high or low (high pitch indicates tension; low pitch, relaxation); does it vary? How does the content influence pitch? The content *ought* to control all. If you see a clear correspondence between content and pitch, in which the preacher allowed the truth to control him rather than confining and conforming content to his own pre-formed speech patterns, you will probably have a sermon worth keeping for further study and possible emulation in the use of voice.

While listening, particularly listen for the use of non-verbal sounds. The preacher who is free enough to make non-verbal noises while preaching in order to better communicate (e.g., oof!, aaah!, clank!, ding-a-ling, etc.) is usually freer in the pulpit than most, and may have much to teach those who have not yet learned much freedom.

Listen too for rate: how fast, how slowly does the preacher speak? Is there good variety? Again, is rate controlled by content? Once more, variety and content control indicate a speaker probably well worth studying from this aspect.

Listen also for volume. Here, of course, the electronic medium will enter in and distort (somewhat) the true picture. But high and low volume with content-controlled variety again can be discovered by careful listening in awareness.[3]

Listen for pulpit pounding—is it appropriate, overdone, altogether absent? How about audience response—laughter? Amens? Other? Here the feedback will tell you something about how well the message was received.

Does the preacher sound excited? Concerned? Moved? Perfunctory? Dull? Uninterested or unconvinced? What does his voice seem to convey?

2. Not complete, but (perhaps) suggestively useful for its clues.
3. Awareness is the key to analysis. Until one knows what elements to look for, all seems to run together.

These elements are adequate for determining whether or not the tape should be filed away for further, more detailed examination as a model. Remember, one man's abilities in the verbal area may not match his content or his stylistic work, so when you file the tape for further study, indicate on the label just where you found the strengths that you wish to examine: e.g., "Strong in illustrative material and rate."

II. *Content Analysis*

If on your initial listenings you think that you have a sermon with exceptional content, then I suggest that you take the time to transcribe it on paper for further analysis.

First, as you do, you will notice the vast difference between good written and good oral English. Good oral English usually looks bad on paper (of course bad oral English can too—so that is not an infallible test!). But we'll come back to that under "stylistic analysis" (use of words, grammar, and syntax).

Here I want to suggest that you ask such questions as: Does the sermon open up a passage of Scripture for the listener? Does the authority of the message stem from clear exposition of the Bible? Does the preacher seem to understand the intention of the Holy Spirit in the passage and constantly pursue it? Do the major points all relate to it? Are there extraneous elements unrelated to the intent of the passage?

Further, ask: Is the introduction compelling—i.e., does it involve the listener in the subject from the outset? Does the conclusion relate directly to the intention of the sermon, and does the preacher leave the listener with the challenge to make the change involved in that intention?

Does the body of the sermon move according to a logical progression? Are there smooth transitions of thought? How well does the preacher argue or state his case? What problems or questions arise in your mind that others are likely to ask? Does he anticipate these too; and answer them?

What about his illustrations? Do they truly illumine his point? Do they make it more vivid, easier to understand or remember? Are they appropriate to what they illustrate? Of what sort are they—short examples or incidents? Longer stories? Well worked out? Do they help? Is there a variety?

Does he use passages of Scripture other than those upon which he is speaking? If so, does he use them well or is there only Bible-flipping? Does he use them to clarify or amplify the preaching passage? Does he briefly but plainly explain them or only cite them?

Is the content abstract or concrete? Applied throughout or only at the end? Does the preacher truly preach about God and the congregation (in the present tense) from the Bible, or does he only lecture *about* Bible characters and events (in the long ago and far away)? Does the listener get involved at the outset and stay involved throughout? Does the exposition of the passage seem inportant to the listener, or is it more suited to the interests of a literary, historical, or grammatical critic?

III. *Stylistic Analysis*

I mentioned the difference between oral English and written English. The first is more concrete, looser, less grammatically exact, more repetitious, more limited in use of vocabulary—especially of technical terms or jargon. Oral English must be comprehended at the speaker's rate—the first time over. Written English can be more compressed and concise. The reader can take it at his pace; stop, think, look up words in the dictionary, etc. The speaker must do all this *for* the listener. So, is this sermon in good oral English—or is it bookish?

Do the words express ideas vividly? With precision? Concretely? Or abstractly? Does he speak about a "car" or a "red '82 Toyota Celica"? Does the preacher overwork terms?

Does the sermon contain vivid description? Is there dialogue? Does it tend to move in the present or in the past? Can you "see," "hear," "taste," "smell," or "feel" what the preacher talks about—is there sense appeal?

Are there climaxes of thought? Does the writer use question clusters at high points? Does he use words that live? Are his verbs active or passive? Is there action? Do his illustrations involve persons in action? If so, are the persons and their actions described in words that make them three dimensional?

All these and other questions should be asked before determining whether you should file away any sermon tape for future study. Be critical; file only good examples; there are so many poor ones. But build (slowly, if necessary) a solid file of tapes that cover all of the above points and study them frequently. Doing so will afford invaluable help that most preachers would be well advised to avail themselves of. One last thought—some of the best examples will be by well-known preachers. But you will find them not *always* strong—or strong at *all points*. And, you will discover some very good preaching in unexpected places among unsung preachers; don't ignore them.

24

THE YOUNG PREACHER

There are many things that veteran preachers can do that are very difficult, if not impossible, for the neophyte. I'd like to make a couple of observations about practices both to avoid and to follow. It is my hope that not only young preachers, but also their longsuffering congregations, will be helped by these suggestions.

One of the unfortunate tendencies evident in many young preachers is the inclination to preach abstractly. Passages full of excitement and flavor are wrung dry as they are twisted and wound into distorted shapes conforming to some plan that is imposed upon them by overzealous, youthful homeliticians who think that abstract and impersonal "points" are superior to normal human speech. This tendency comes from poor teaching in the seminaries, from the sort of dull materials to which seminarians have been exposed for three or more years, and from the perversity of youth who think that this is the way to become sophisticated. As the result, congregations are fed a regular diet of

    I. The Nature of Truth (or whatever)
   II. The Necessity of Truth
  III. The Negative of Truth

As you readily can see, abstraction is not the only problem apparent in this outline. But, for a moment, let us stick with the abstraction problem. Instead of those boring and drab labels, "Nature" and "Necessity," why not simply say

  I. Jesus is the Truth
 II. Jesus wants you to speak the truth, etc.?

You will say more; and as you do you will say it directly, *preaching* (even in your "points") to the congregation rather than merely *analyzing* a "subject."

Doubtless, you have also noted that the penchant for alliteration that so many young preachers exhibit has led the youthful minister who composed the outline into bad practices. He squeezed into the outline point three, "The Negative of Truth," even though it really didn't fit, just to get another "N." Neither the structure of the phrase nor the word "Negative" is apropos. What he meant to say was something like this: Look at the opposite, or (to continue our substitute outline)

III. Jesus wants you to stop lying.

How often young men (and some older ones—watch out for preachers who always alliterate), enamored with alliteration, force the meaning of a passage for the sake of alliteration! Let me warn you that alliteration is useful *only* when it is natural, when it helps one to remember, and when it clearly says what you want to say. Then it really can be useful. But any alliteration that distorts meaning *always must be avoided*.

Another related problem that young preachers have is the desire to preach abstract rather than concrete passages of Scripture. While the whole Bible must be preached, it cannot all be preached at once. Because that is true, the preacher must pick and choose the portions of Scripture from which he is going to preach. When he does so, the inexperienced preacher will be wise to choose those passages that by virtue of their form and content already have a lot of interest value in them, that are fairly extensive in length (rather than single verses or parts of verses), and that have in them people in action and in conversation. He would be well advised to preach from a number of the parables, miracles, and healings of Christ. Because of the way in which Luke handles these events (giving suggestive details and focusing on people, I recommend that the young preacher get as many commentaries as he can afford on the Gospel of Luke (and perhaps borrow a few more from others' libraries) and preach largely (though not exclusively) from this Gospel for the first couple of years.

25

A SUGGESTION FOR YOUNG PREACHERS

Recently listening to a young man who has great promise preach, I was reminded afresh of a fact of which I became aware early in my teaching of homiletics at Westminster Theological Seminary:

> *Young preachers—and some older ones too—tend to preach too much in a sermon.*

The sermon to which I refer ranged far and wide, over Old Testament and New, into various doctrines and their subpoints, all (mind you) in 25 minutes! Apparently, the young man had never considered the fact that *you can say more about less.*

Were I to attempt to describe the activities in which I was engaged last summer in 25 minutes, I'd be saying such things as

> Then I went to several other places (I wish I had time to tell you where and all about them) and did some very interesting things (perhaps at some later time I could mention these in detail), etc.

But, if I took 25 minutes to tell you about one event on one night at one place last summer, I could tell all—colorfully, interestingly, and in a way that you could understand. Instead of hurriedly racing hither and yon, I could stop, examine in detail, describe in depth, delineate, and delete. But all of last summer? Why, all I could do is vaguely sketch what took place!

The same is true of preaching. The young man had a decently chosen preaching portion, but, instead of delving into it, he ran all over the Bible. He should have explored its main *telos* (purpose) in depth, related it carefully to the contemporary scene, and sent us away with one whale of an impact from the Word of God. Instead, we went out barely touched by it. His effort was dissipated by scattering his shot. Someone has said, "A rifle is more powerful than a shotgun."

So, let's stop using birdshot in the pulpit.

Now, for my suggestion. Preachers are always looking for ways to reuse old sermons. That is OK: New Testament preachers did. But here is one of the best ways of all. Review your first three to five years' sermons. You will notice that (if you are like most novices) you tried to preach the entire corpus of Christian truth in every message.

"OK," you say, "I've looked at them (shudder!), and the charge is true. What do I do now?" My suggestion is this:

Use each of the three to five points in each sermon, itself, as the basis for a complete sermon. Perhaps some points could be so fully elaborated (remember, you can say more about less) that they could form the basis for a series of sermons.

There, you have it. Take it to heart. Don't dump those old, unusable sermons in the wastebasket. There is some valuable ore there to be mined. Go to it, now that you know how!

Preaching to the Heart

*To Jim Baird,
preacher to
the heart*

1
Introduction

For years homileticians have been exhorting preachers to "preach to the heart." But what are they talking about? Do you know? Do *they*? Is the concept biblical, and if so, how does one do it? These and similar questions often remain unanswered, and the typical preacher goes on doing what he always has done, resigned to the assumption that says, "I'll never be a great preacher; I guess I'll never be able to preach to the heart."

Is that true? Does the capacity for preaching to the heart belong only to the exceptionally gifted? Or is it rather that preaching to the heart is a developed skill that makes preachers great? The whole concept has been presented in such a vague and fuzzy way that anyone unfamiliar with it would find it difficult or impossible to obey the injunction.

The blame for confusion about what it means to "preach to the heart" does not lie solely with homileticians, while preachers go off scot-free. Homileticians should make themselves clear. But if they don't, it is the responsibility of the preachers to pound on their doors until they do. So neither is guiltless. There has been a conspiracy of ignorance in which words and phrases have been uttered again and again as though the speakers and the listeners knew perfectly well what they were talking about, when all the while they did not. As a homiletician who has been at fault in this matter, I believe something must be done. It is time the whole matter were cleared up. That is the point of this book.

My purpose is to show that preaching to the heart is biblical and therefore necessary, and that any man with the gifts and heart for preaching can be taught clearly how to do it. Indeed, I propose to go even further: in the pages that follow I shall endeavor to teach him how to do so.

The Concept Is Biblical

The first Christian sermon, preached on the day of Pentecost by the apostle Peter, was preached to the heart. Luke wrote:

> Now when they heard this, they were stung[1] to the heart and said to Peter and the rest of the apostles, "Brothers, what should we do?" (Acts 2:37).

That crowd response was the fruit of effective preaching, empowered by the Holy Spirit. But effective, heart-penetrating preaching can also lead to the opposite response:

> Now when they heard these things, they were pierced through[2] to their hearts and gnashed their teeth at him (Acts 7:54).

When Peter preached, great numbers repented and believed the gospel; when Stephen preached, his listeners killed him. Yet both were filled with the Spirit and preached to the heart. This double and opposite response makes one thing clear at the outset: while preaching to the heart is a desirable effect brought about by the power of the Spirit, the exact nature of that effect on the listener may vary greatly and cannot be predicted beforehand.

In either case, Spirit empowered, biblical preaching strikes squarely at the heart. It elicits a response. No hearer can remain apathetic: *he must respond.* To speak of preaching to the heart, then, is to speak of preaching that brings a definitive response; it is preaching that evokes words and action from the listener.

Think of it—preaching that calls forth action! Preaching that gets results! Preaching that so stirs the listener that he must respond! That is what we need today.

Is there any reader who wouldn't like to preach or hear preaching like that? Is there any reader who *has* heard much preaching like that? Something is wrong; what has happened to our preaching? Why is that sort of preaching virtually unknown? That too we must investigate and decide what God wants us to do about it.

---

1. The verb, *katanusso*, is a strong term that means "to prick, to stun, to smite, to sting." This compound word is a combination of *nusso*, "to pierce, to puncture," and *kata*, a prepositional prefix that intensifies the action. The passive of the verb connotes being pricked or stung to the heart.
2. The verb *diaprio*, here translated "pierced through," is also used in Acts 5:33. It has in it the idea of "sawing through" (*prio* = "to saw, sever, bite," and *dia* = "through") and often carries the meaning of "cutting (through) to the heart."

2
What Is the Heart?

A clear idea of what the Bible means by *heart* is foundational to all else that we shall consider in this little book. Indeed, the widespread careless use of that word is responsible for the confusion and vagueness that surround exhortations to preach to the heart.

"But," you object, "everyone knows what *heart* means. I don't see why you are making such a fuss over it. Surely it doesn't take an entire chapter to define something so obvious, does it?" Yes. You see, that's exactly what is wrong: everyone thinks he understands the term, but very few do. Ask yourself, "Exactly what does the word *heart* mean in the *Scriptures?*" Can you give a precise definition? "Well, maybe not an exact one, but I know what it means, nevertheless."

Do you?

Let's test your understanding a bit, okay? What do you think of the often quoted sentiment, "What we need is more heart knowledge and not just head knowledge"? Do you think it does or does not convey an acceptable idea of *heart* as the word is used in the Bible?

"Well, I guess so, but I'm not sure; anyhow, I know what the sentence is getting at."

What?

"It is saying that it isn't enough to merely know truth, that truth must grip you—it has to affect your emotions as well."

You are probably correct about the way that sentence is used; but the fact is, it suggests an incorrect interpretation of the biblical word *heart*. If *heart* is used to refer to feelings or emotions as over against thought or intellect, that use is discordant with Scripture. Never in the Bible is the word *heart* set over against the head or the intellectual processes. That is a modern, Western idea of the heart, introduced into the Bible from the outside. One would never get that idea from the Bible itself. Indeed, that is a Roman rather than a biblical view of the heart. The Valentine's Day cupid, shooting arrows through little red or pink hearts, is the culprit behind this modern, unbiblical view. To Western origins may be attributed all of our romantic notions, which include the idea of heart-as-feeling. No such conception can be found in the Scriptures.

Consider instead what *is* contrasted with the word *heart* in the Bible. In Matthew 15:8, for instance, we read that the people honor God "with their lips, but their heart is far from" Him. That sort of contrast is regularly made in the Scriptures. You find the same thing in the well-known passage in Romans 10 in which we are told that it is not enough to confess Christ with the mouth; the one making the profession also must believe in his heart. Notice the contrast: heart/lips, heart/mouth. In the important passage I Samuel 16:7 we are assured that "man looks on the outward appearances but [in contrast] God looks on the heart." Plainly, in all of these pivotal passages there is a contrast between the heart as something inner and the lips, mouth, and appearance as something outer. That is the true biblical contrast; not a contrast between intellect and emotion.

But what is this inner and outer man? The inner is called the "hidden person of the heart" in I Peter 3:4. The inner person is the one that the Lord alone knows—he is hidden from us; we look only at the outer man. That is one major reason why we must never judge a man's motives: we simply don't know what they are. Rather, we must judge only his actions and his words (i.e., those factors that *are* accessible to us).

The outer man is the manifest person, the one we are familiar with; the inner man is the person known only to God and, in part, to himself. This inner man is not his feelings. In the Bible the notion of feelings is expressed by the word for viscera; we read, for instance, of *"bowels* of compassion." Clearly, the heart includes the whole inner man—the intellect along with the emotions as well. In the 14th Psalm there is a good example of the intellectual use where we are told that "The fool says in his heart that there is no God " (Ps. 14:1). Incidentally, he is a fool because he listens to one!¹ Here we see the fool involved in an intellectual process: talking himself into a false belief. And so it goes throughout the Bible. In various passages people are said to reason, plan, understand, think, doubt, perceive, make mistakes, purpose, intend, and the like *in their hearts!* One of the ways to say that a person lacks good sense is to say (translating literally) that he "lacks heart" (cf. Prov. 9:4, 16). Clearly, then, in the Bible the word *heart* does not mean emotion.

With that false interpretation out of the way, we are prepared to ask what the word *heart* does mean as it refers to the inner man. It has several ideas folded together. *Heart* means good sense, as we have just seen, but it also means conscience (cf. Heb. 10:22; I John 3:9-21). It is the "treasure house" (Luke 6:45) from which one's actions and words flow. Putting these and other concepts of *heart* together we come to the conclusion that the heart is the inner life one lives before God and himself.² It is the source of the outer life (Matt. 15:19), and it expresses more certainly what a person is really like than what he does or says externally. That is why God "tries the heart." Thus to do something "from the heart" is to do it genuinely. And to do it "with all your heart" is to do it wholeheartedly rather than with a "double" or divided heart.

A hypocrite is one who focuses on being "seen of men" rather than being seen by God; he pretends by his outward show of holiness to be something that, inwardly, he is not. It is possible to sin in the heart without committing any outward offense (Matt. 5:28). Only one person in the history of the world ever had both heart and outer appearance completely in sync at all times—Jesus Christ. The rest of us, as sinners, have various inconsistencies between the inner and outer life.

The word *heart* has become a devalued currency in our culture. Preachers too often read the modern Western view of heart-as-emotional-commitment back into Scripture and thus mistake and distort what the Holy Spirit moved the writers of the Bible to say.

---

1. The fool, *nabal,* is not only one who is stupid, but one who is wicked and boorish. The Hebrew word refers to a falling leaf or a withered fruit. It has the notion of something useless, bad, abandoned and full of weakness and decay.

2. For a fuller discussion of the word, see my book, *More than Redemption* (Phillipsburg, N.J.: Presbyterian and Reformed Publishing Co., 1979).

It is time to restore the true biblical content of the word so that we may profit from an understanding of those many passages in which it occurs.

If the heart of man in the Bible refers to the inner life, from which all else flows, what is the point of preaching to the heart? In the light of this meaning, we may say that preaching that goes to the heart genuinely affects the person. He has been hit at the very source of his whole life (Prov. 4:23). He has been pierced by the preached Word where it counts. This does not necessarily mean that he is converted or, in the case of a believer, that he will repent of his sin, but it does mean that the sermon has truly hit home. That is why, whether the response is favorable or unfavorable, preaching that pierces the heart is preaching that elicits a response. It could not do otherwise because, as we have just seen, the heart is the source of every response. It also may be said that preaching that penetrates or cuts through to the heart is preaching that elicits a *genuine* response—whether it be faith or fury. Preaching that gets through to the heart does not leave the listener apathetic.

In contrast, preaching that does not go to the heart of a man is preaching without any genuine effect. While the listener may express gratitude for the help he has received, the words on his lips do not flow from heartfelt conviction. In time, his speech and actions will reflect the true condition of his heart. "By their fruits shall you know them." When the inner man is truly affected by the Word for good, that will lead to a positive, lasting change in his outward behavior. The outer and inner man will come into closer sync through discernible patterns of growth.

So, you can see how desirable it is to preach to the heart. Indeed, a strong biblical case could be made that unless preaching penetrates deeply enough to affect the inner life, it is not preaching at all. True biblical preaching changes people. It did in Bible times, and there is no reason why it will not do so today. We possess the same Spirit and the same Word by which and from which they preached. The only difference is that they preached to the heart and we so often do not. We must discover the causes of this failure in present-day preaching and apply the biblical cure.

3
Two Kinds of Hearts

When the Word of God is preached, it receives two kinds of responses: some hearts are "hardened," and others are transformed. What is the reason for this difference and what does it mean to the preacher of the Word?

First, note that these two responses are everywhere distinguished in the Bible itself. In the two verses from Acts mentioned in the introduction, we see the two responses in the plainest contrast. Although both Peter and Stephen preached in the power of the Holy Spirit, and the words of both penetrated their listeners' hearts, the responses to their preaching were exactly opposite: Peter's preaching resulted in many conversions, while Stephen's preaching infuriated his listeners, at the cost of his life. Luke's description of Stephen as a "man full of the Holy Spirit and faith" (Acts 6:5; see also 6:3, 10, 15, as well as 7:55, 56) makes it clear that neither his attitude nor his preaching was to blame for the negative response.[1] While preaching to the heart invariably gets results—either hot or cold, never lukewarm—there's no telling beforehand what the result will be.

Let's take a closer look at Acts 2:37 and 7:54, which I quoted in full in the introduction. In Acts 2:37 the crowd was "stung to the heart" by Peter's Pentecostal sermon, and in Acts 7:54, the result of Stephen's preaching was that members of the Sanhedrin were "pierced through to their hearts." Moreover, both sermons elicited action from those who heard: in the first instance, the listen-

---

1. Stifler, in his all-but-forgotten, yet extremely valuable, book, *An Introduction to the Study of the Acts of the Apostles,* makes a strong case for the direct inspiration of these early sermons in Acts. Whether he is correct or not, they do set before us a valuable pattern for preaching. But, how much more so if he is right (the idea here is that they were the fulfillment of Luke 21:12-15).

ers asked, "What shall we do?"; in the second, they "gnashed their teeth" and picked up stones to kill Stephen.

As I have pointed out, the difference in results stemmed not from the preachers themselves, or the types of sermons they preached, or the manner in which they preached; both preached under the full approval and power of the Holy Spirit, who expressly played a prominent part in both events. No, only one factor can account for the difference—the hearts of those who heard the Word.

Both groups heard the Word. Both took it to heart. In the first instance, Peter's message is said to have "stung" the heart. The word translated "stung" is *katanusso,* a Greek term that may also be translated "to strike or prick violently, to stun or to smite." Clearly, the word speaks of a strong impact or powerful jolt on the inner life. In the second instance, a different word is employed to describe the effect of Stephen's preaching on the Pharisees. It is *diaprio,* a word meaning "to saw asunder, or cut through to" as well as "pierce through." Again, this very forceful word describes an act in which all barriers to hearing have been penetrated. In both Peter's preaching and Stephen's, the heart was reached. But only in the first instance was the heart changed. Though in the second, the heart was strongly affected, it remained unchanged and responded negatively to the Word. So while preaching to the heart always *reaches the heart*—the inner man—and has impact on it, one heart receives God's Word and is altered by it for good, whereas another hears it, rejects it, and turns on the one who preaches.

The Bible affirms throughout that there are two different sorts of hearts. In Ezekiel 36:16 we read about a "heart of stone" and a "heart of flesh." Peter's message was received by the latter, Stephen's by the former. The heart of flesh is warm and living, responsive to God's Word, while the heart of stone is dead and unresponsive. The difference is seen again and again. For instance, in Hebrews 6, a passage that some have found troublesome because it talks about professed Christians falling away (v. 6), the answer to the supposed problem is that, in time, those who have a heart of stone will manifest the fact as, indeed, those with hearts of flesh will; the first will fall away and the second will not. The passage does not teach that those who have good hearts will fall away, but only those whose hearts are stony. That is clear from verses 7-9, in which the two diverse sorts of hearts are referred to under the figure of two types of ground. Both receive the same rain—i.e., both have had the very same influences, including the preaching of the Word (cf. v. 6)—but the results in each type of ground are different. The one ground brings forth fruit, the other weeds. Clearly, the different responses to heavenly influences are due not to any difference in preaching (the rain is the same) but to differences in the hearts of the ones who hear it. In one case the Word is mixed with faith, while in the other it is not (cf. Heb. 4:2). So, the reason why the response to Peter's sermon was faith and the response to Stephen's was fury is that God's rain fell on two distinct types of ground.

There are many other examples in Scripture. Paul, for instance, has a lot to say about distinct types of hearts, in I Corinthians 2. In verse 14 he asserts, "But a natural person doesn't welcome the teachings of God's Spirit; they are foolishness to him, and he isn't able to know about them because they must be investigated spiritually." Here, the person with the stony heart is called a "natural person." He is the person to whom nothing *super*natural has ever happened. He came into this world "dead in trespasses and sins," with a nature that is both corrupt and guilty before God, and nothing since has changed that picture. The natural person is in darkness because he has inherited a nature from Adam that is dead toward God and the teachings of His Spirit. He has no heart for God or the things of God. The spiritual person, also mentioned in this passage, is the person who has a heart of flesh. Something supernatural has happened to him: his old heart has been replaced and the Spirit of God now dwells in his inner life, enabling him to understand and otherwise respond positively to God's Word as it is preached.

The room in which you sit is full of sights and sounds, many of which you selectively block out of your mind. In the same way, the natural person, while surrounded by a vast display of God's glory, covers his eyes and ears to the many evidences for God's goodness. Indeed, he may show hostility whenever they are mentioned to him (especially if they are driven home to his heart). Paul puts it this way: "What eye hasn't seen and the ear hasn't heard, and what hasn't been conceived by the human heart is what God has prepared for those who love Him" (v. 9). The "human heart" is the heart as it is in its natural, unregenerate state. It is, as Isaiah said, a heart that has "grown thick," one that cannot "understand" (Acts 28:27), the heart over which a veil lies (II Cor. 3:15); it will not respond favorably to God's Word until its "blindness" has been removed, so that the light of God's truth about Christ may shine in (II Cor. 4:4-6).

Paul has made it plain that the things of God are prepared for and *"given"* (I Cor. 2:10) to "those who love Him." But the natural, stony heart has no love for God. That love must be "poured into our hearts through the Holy Spirit" as He is "given" (Rom. 5:5). Indeed, as Paul elsewhere asserts, "nobody can say, 'Jesus is Lord,' except by the Holy Spirit "(I Cor. 12:3). It is in the giving of the Spirit that the new heart is given.

Since preaching to the heart is a matter of preaching to two different sorts of hearts, that distinction must be understood. Not that we must know *which* kind of heart we face. When Peter and Stephen preached, neither knew which kind of heart he was preaching to. God does not give us the right or the ability to look into other men's hearts; He reserves that privilege for Himself. Our task is to preach the Word effectively, so that it penetrates to the hearts of men; God opens the hearts to the preached Word as He sovereignly determines. Hearts are closed to God's truth until He opens them. Of Lydia it is written that "the Lord opened her heart to pay attention to what Paul said" (Acts 16:14). It is He who gives the "new heart" of "flesh" and removes the "heart of stone" (Ezek. 36:26). Again, according to this passage in Ezekiel, that happens only when God puts His Spirit in a man. Regeneration is God's work; the preacher regenerates no one. God Himself must "quicken," or give life to, those who are "dead in trespasses and sins" (Eph. 2). That life, that new heart, enables one to understand and believe the message when it reaches the heart. The heart is the soil upon which the seed is sown; if it is good soil, it will bring forth fruit; if not, there will be no harvest.

4
Preaching from the Heart

How does one preach to the heart? In several chapters, I shall consider that question biblically. But, any answer must begin with the observation that to preach to the heart one must preach *from the heart.*

What do I mean by that? Simply this: a preacher of God's Word must be genuine. His inner belief and desire must correspond to the words he speaks. Another way to say the same thing is to say that he must be filled with the Holy Spirit. The Holy Spirit fills those who are genuine and gives them power to preach effectively. The powerful impact of the sermons of Peter and Stephen[1] can be accounted for in no other way than to say that the Holy Spirit was at work as they preached.

Consider what Luke wrote about Stephen: "But they couldn't stand up against the wisdom and the Spirit with which he spoke" (Acts 6:10). Calvin, commenting on this passage, says: "They could not resist the wisdom which the Spirit of God gave him. . . . the enemies of the gospel were therefore discouraged and overcome, because they did strive against the Spirit of God, which spake by the mouth of Stephen. And forasmuch as Christ hath promised the same Spirit to all his servants, let us only defend the truth faithfully, and let us crave a mouth and wisdom of him, and we shall be sufficiently furnished to speak. . . ." Stephen was a man in whom the Spirit was at work; such men preach to the heart, because they preach from the heart. That

---

1. Stephen's sermon must not be considered a failure because of the results. The failure was on the part of his listeners. Not only was it a success in God's sight because it exposed their sin, but it became the occasion for a persecution that pushed the gospel out of Palestine, where it had been bottled up, toward the ends of the earth.

heart is a heart dominated by the Spirit.

What does it mean to be *filled with the Spirit?* In that phrase, the idea of domination is uppermost. When the Bible speaks of being filled with amazement, with fear, with jealousy, or with joy, similarly, the idea of domination is in view. A person who is filled with fear is dominated by fear; everything he does or says in that condition is colored by fear. His voice, his actions, his decisions, everything is under the influence of this dominant emotion. The same is true of one who is "filled" with jealousy, joy, or amazement.[2]

The important passage in which we are *commanded* to be filled with the Spirit (Eph. 5:18) sets up an informative contrast between the Spirit and wine. Wine dominates the drunkard so that all he does is under its influence; similarly, Paul says, the Holy Spirit's influence must dominate the whole of one's life.

How does the Spirit fill, dominate, or exert such total influence? Don't think of the Spirit's filling in terms of pumping gasoline into your automobile tank. Rather, the image of the church auditorium better fits the situation. When the church is "filled," every seat is taken. When a drunkard is filled with wine, every part of his life is affected by it, every area is under the influence of wine. It destroys his home life, his social life, his physical life, his business life. That is why Paul wrote, "Do not be drunk with wine *which leads to utter ruin*" (the word for utter ruin is *asotia,* "unsavableness, beyond salvaging"). Paul warns of utter ruin, because there is nothing that escapes wine's influence; wine destroys *all* of the drunkard's life—there is nothing left untouched that may be salvaged. Similarly, when a person is filled with the Spirit, every aspect of his life is under the Spirit's influence; there are no areas that are untouched by Him. That does not mean the person filled with the Spirit is perfect, but it does mean that the Spirit is at work in the totality of his life. Preachers who preach to the heart are men who preach under the influence of the Spirit.

Preachers whose lives are filled with the Spirit are genuine; they are not hypocrites who lose preaching power because they harbor sin in certain areas of their lives. Because they too have

---

2. According to Luke, a life under Satan's influence also can be said to be "filled": "Why has Satan filled your heart to lie to the Holy Spirit . . . ?" (Acts 5:3a).

been dealing with sin in all areas of their lives, they understand the problems of those to whom they preach. They preach with conviction because there is no area of life about which they fear to speak lest their preaching boomerang. They have already acknowledged their need for the Spirit to transform them totally and are asking Him to do so. Because they hold nothing back, they can preach with abandon. Moreover, having already experienced something of the Spirit's pruning in every aspect of life, they are able to zero in on their listeners' problems in ways that could not be learned from textbooks alone. That too makes a difference in the way they preach.

If there is one emphasis found in the Book of Acts, it is the church's power in preaching and that this power came from the filling of the Holy Spirit. There is no other way to explain the church's rapid growth. Times have changed, and so has preaching. But our God has not. Neither He nor the needs of men have been changed by the passing of time; sin and salvation, repentance and sanctification all remain the same. What has changed is that preachers today believe they do not need the filling of the Spirit, have a distorted view of what that filling is, or do not think it is possible. It is time we begin to reexamine the biblical teaching on the subject; then, perhaps, we would begin to experience power in our lives and in our preaching.

This filling of the Spirit is not some second work of grace. Rather, it is an ongoing work in which the Spirit more and more controls each area of our lives. It is the sanctification (the gradual process of putting off sin and replacing it with righteousness) of the whole man. It is a matter of asking the Spirit to work in every area of life, and a willingness to be changed by Him in anything, no matter what it may be. This is what Paul prayed for the Thessalonians: "May the God of peace Himself sanctify you completely; may your entire being—spirit and soul and body—be kept blameless for the coming of our Lord Jesus Christ" (I Thess. 5:23).

The original worshipers on the day of Pentecost, together with those converted on that occasion, were genuinely Spirit filled: "Every day they continued to meet in the temple in unity of spirit, and from house to house they broke bread together, sharing meals in gladness and *sincerity of heart.*" They were *genuine.* It is not as though only the apostles and elders were filled with the

Spirit; all who were present when the Spirit fell were filled (Acts 2:4). Yet, later on when the church wanted men fit to become deacons, it was necessary to "look for" men with "a good reputation, full of the Spirit and wisdom" (Acts 6:3). Presumably, by that time, not every believer was manifesting such a domination of the Spirit as all did at Pentecost (Acts 2:4), and so there was need to discriminate between those who were filled with the Spirit and those who were not.

It would seem that the original Pentecostal filling of the Spirit was an immediate, complete domination of the Spirit that caught up the 120 for that important occasion. But, the Spirit's fullness was not to be automatically maintained. Pentecost was special; today, filling does not occur as an instant event in which we are passive. Rather, it is commanded (Eph. 5:18), indicating that we play a part in the process, and the verb in that verse makes it clear that filling is not a once-for-all event,[3] but must be nurtured by one's relationship to Christ. That is why, even by the time of Acts 6, it could be said that deacons must be selected only from among those who were filled with the Spirit (implying that not all were).

Tragically, today it cannot be said of every preacher in conservative churches (let alone deacons, elders, or members), that he is filled with the Spirit. This is the first problem. We must preach from the heart—a heart dominated by the Spirit—if we would preach to the hearts of others. But to preach from such a heart means that inwardly, day by day, we must experience the sanctifying work of the Spirit in every area of our lives. Preachers who do not preach with power to the hearts of men, therefore, should first examine their own hearts to be sure that the words of Peter and John addressed to Simon are not also appropriate to them: "You have no part or share in the proclamation of this message because your heart isn't right before God" (Acts 8:21). Clearly, all who wish to preach are not qualified to do so; the Word is to be proclaimed only by those whose hearts are right before God. Preaching is a heart-to-heart matter. When one's heart is right before God and he is a man after God's heart, he will be able to preach from heart to heart. Men like that will preach like the preachers in the Book of Acts.

3. The tense of the verb in Ephesians 5:18, *plerousthe,* indicates a continual process, not a one-time or once-for-all event.

5
Boldness of Heart

We are considering the question, "How does one preach to the heart?," and we have discovered thus far that the precondition for such preaching is a heart that is right with God. Power in preaching is an index of the fact that the preacher is filled with the Spirit. Only those whose hearts are right before God have any part in the proclamation of God's Word. Those who preach to the hearts of others, therefore, are those who have experienced the penetrating power of the sword of the Spirit thrust into their own hearts. They preach out of hearts that are dominated and influenced by the Spirit of God. They are preachers whose own hearts are aflame.

What does this do for a preacher? It gives him boldness in preaching.

If there is one characteristic that typifies modern preaching, it is its insipid, obsequious approach to speaking the truth. So unlike the early preachers, the Reformers, and the great preachers of all time, many modern Bible-believing preachers seem afraid to tell it like it is. And yet, that modern phrase, "tell it like it is," indicates that people generally appreciate hearing truth for what it is, even when what they hear isn't altogether pleasant. But it seems that in Christian circles, in particular, there is a pseudo-pious reserve or oversophistication in which hypersensitive listeners are horrified by anything frank in preaching. There is, therefore, something wrong with modern preaching, and many of those who have been brought up on it, that must be corrected. It is basically a willingness to compromise—even God's truth—which stems from a lack of boldness.

I am not commending rudeness or crudeness. These unnecessary characteristics are often assumed to be synonymous with boldness. But there is nothing rude or crude about the preaching in the Book of Acts. The preaching found there is straightforward, clear, explicit, hard hitting, and, in short, bold. In fact, the only feature of apostolic preaching described in Acts is its boldness.

Let's take a look at what Luke says about this matter and then at some of the preaching itself. The classic statement on the subject is found in the fourth chapter of Acts. There, the apostles and the people pray,

> ". . . So now, Lord, take note of their threats and give your slaves all the boldness needed to speak Your word" (Acts 4:29).

Verse 31 indicates that the prayer was answered and that they "spoke God's word boldly."

Even before this time, Luke notes that there was already a boldness about apostolic preaching that struck those who heard:

> Now when they saw the boldness of Peter and John and realized that they were uneducated laymen, they were surprised and recognized that they had been with Jesus (Acts 4:13).

Boldness, then, was considered a prerequisite for preaching and, when seen, was noted favorably. The same is true today, no less than it was in apostolic times: boldness is essential for preaching to the heart, and bold preaching makes an impact on those who hear.

It was said that when they saw the boldness of Peter and John, they recognized that "they had been with Jesus." The way some prissy Christians today look aghast at any boldness in preaching, you would think instead that a bold preacher had been with the devil! Most people, however, recognize a truly bold preacher as an unusual man and are interested in him and often in what he has to say. One reason why much contemporary preaching not only fails to reach the heart, but is so uninteresting, is that it is timid and pale. Bold preaching is never dull.

What is boldness? The Greek word, *parresia*, means freedom in speaking, openness, willingness to be frank; it is plain speech that is unencumbered by fear. A bold preacher is one who has no fear of speaking the truth—even when it hurts. Many ministries are hampered today simply because of the fear of men. "Will Mrs. Jones take offense if I preach this?," "What will happen if I teach this to the congregation?," and similar thoughts go through the minds of far too many preachers, when what they ought to be asking themselves is, "What will God think of me if I don't teach His truth?"

There is far too little teaching about judgment, hell, and the other doctrines on the dark side of the scriptural spectrum. There is too little reproving of sin. There is too little church discipline and confronting error, even when it is seriously affecting the membership of the church. There is a fear of controversy.

In some circles, the fear of controversy is so great that preachers, and congregations following after them, will settle for peace at any cost—even at the cost of truth, God's truth. The idea is that peace is all-important. Peace is a biblical ideal (Rom. 12:18 makes that clear: "If possible, so far as it depends on you, be at peace with everybody."[1]) but so is purity. The peace of the church may never be bought at the cost of the purity of the church. That price is too dear. But why do we think that we can get along in this world, or for that matter, even in that church, without conflict and controversy? Jesus didn't. Paul didn't. None of the preachers of the apostolic age who faithfully served their Lord were spared controversy. Who are we to escape controversy when they did not? The story of the advance of the church across the Mediterranean world from Jerusalem to Rome is a story of controversy. When the gospel is preached boldly, there will be controversy. Most of the Epistles themselves were called forth to counter error of doctrine and sinfulness of life. In them there is controversy. The life of Paul is a life of controversy. Tradition tells us that every apostle except John, who was exiled for his faith, died a violent death.

What is this hypersensitivity that is so often found among a particular brand of evangelicals today? Children around us grow up on TV and movies that feature not only conflict, but violence and crudity. Who in our age is so allergic to frankness that the open preaching of God's Word will cause him to break out in

---

1. The words, "if possible," show Paul's realism. Intransigent unbelief and disobedience on the part of others may make peace impossible when they hold out for what opposes God.

horror? Pale, insipid preaching is what drives people from Christ and the church, not bold preaching. It seems to me that the problem with hypersensitive evangelicals is not really the one stated up front—offending those to whom we preach—but, more often than not, simply a lack of boldness. And that lack of boldness boils down to a simple fear of men—fear of the consequences of telling it like it is.

Preachers are soldiers in a battle for Christ, Paul told Timothy. As faithful soldiers, fighting the good fight, they are to assault the walls of thought that men rear up against the gospel and take captives for Christ. They are also shepherds. As good shepherds, they are to drive wolves away from the flock and rescue those sheep that wander into dangerous places. A good shepherd carries not only a staff, but a rod (a mace used to drive off wild animals) and a sling (remember David's?). The images of the pastor/preacher are not images of men in soft clothing who never soil their hands; they are images of the hard-working farmer in his struggle against weeds, the soldier fighting the enemy, the shepherd protecting the sheep: they are images of conflict. If a minister of the gospel is afraid to "fight the good fight," he does not "keep the faith." So, in order to discharge his duties faithfully, he must be bold.

Boldness characterized the preaching of the apostles and other early preachers, Luke says. Let's take just a brief glimpse at a bit of their preaching. When the 3,000 were stung in their hearts, what sort of preaching was it that led to that? First of all, we see that it was preaching that did not hesitate to contradict the expressed ideas of men. Some said that the 120 who were speaking in foreign languages were drunk. But when Peter got up to preach, the very first words out of his mouth contradicted this foolish accusation: "Certainly these people aren't drunk, as you imagine; it's only nine o'clock in the morning!" (Acts 2:15). Well-meaning and fearful preachers will tell you that to openly contradict the audience is a poor preaching tactic—especially at the beginning of a sermon! But Peter had not read the experts; he simply relied on the Holy Spirit and went ahead speaking the truth. To win friends and influence people, you are supposed to begin by gaining agreement. But Peter was more interested in the truth than in manipulating people by selling techniques.

Not only did Peter begin all wrong, according to the experts, but he was far too frank when he discussed his congregation's behavior. After all, Peter, it isn't polite to say such things as "this Man, delivered up by God's predetermined plan and foreknowledge, you killed by crucifixion!" (Acts 2:23). That sounds like a direct accusation, if not an attack on the audience. You'll never get anywhere that way, Peter. But Peter isn't finished. Listen to the conclusion: "So then, let the whole house of Israel know for certain that God has made this Jesus Whom you crucified both Lord and Christ." Now there you've done it, Peter! Just when it looked as if you might have pulled your sermon out of the fire after that opening blunder, you went ahead and spoiled everything by adding that last dig, "Whom you crucified." And, while I'm at it, let me tell you something else, Peter. You will never get anywhere using the second person in preaching; it's too personal. It is possible that you might have gotten away with saying everything you said—even those all-too-frank accusations—if you had only phrased them in the third person, in a more abstract way.

Now will Peter listen to reason? No, there he is in Acts 3, once again slinging around the second person and accosting his hearers with words like these: "Whom you delivered over and denied in front of Pilate . . ." (Acts 3:13b); "But you denied the Holy and Righteous One and asked for a murderer to be given to you . . ." (Acts 3:14); "So you killed the Author of life . . ." (Acts 3:15a). Peter, that sort of preaching certainly isn't calculated to win sermon prizes!

Well, when we listen to him in Acts 4, we see that Peter is never satisfied, never learns. There he is, at it again, as usual, using the second person and telling people in his typical, brassy manner how they have sinned : "Let all of you and all of the people of Israel know that it is by the name of Jesus Christ the Nazarene, Whom you crucified . . ." (Acts 4:10).

I guess it's hopeless trying to get anything across to Peter; and we won't even mention Stephen, with his aggressiveness: "You stiffnecked people, uncircumcised in hearts and ears! You always resist the Holy Spirit. As your fathers did, so do you! . . . they killed those who predicted the coming of the righteous One, of Whom you now have become the murderers and betrayers . . ."

(Acts 7:51, 52,). No, Stephen also is hopeless.

So, let's try Paul; he's a highly educated man. Can we expect a more refined approach from him? I'm not sure we are going to get very far there either. Look how he begins his preaching: "he preached boldly in Jesus' name . . . going in and out, preaching boldly in the Lord's name" (Acts 9:27, 28). We've already seen what this boldness is like! Perhaps he will do better on his first missionary journey. Oh my, listen to him at Paphos, the very first place where we hear what he has to say: "You son of the devil, full of every kind of deceit and fraud, you enemy of every kind of righteousness; won't you ever stop making the Lord's straight roads crooked?" (Acts 13:10).[2] Paul, that won't do. That sort of talk will get you in all sorts of trouble; why you might be thrown into prison, or beaten, or even stoned!"

I won't go further. To do so would only multiply the obvious. Apostolic preachers were clear, personal, and direct; they were fearless. At times they were bold to the point of being blunt. Today, we need to be reminded of this. There is no denying the fact that, on the whole, today's mild preaching is very different; one might even call it antiseptic, by comparison. And so too are the results quite different. The reason for these differences is that today preachers lack boldness of heart.

As we have seen, the early church prayed for boldness, and the Spirit produced this boldness within them (Acts 4:29-31). That is the same way that preachers must acquire boldness today. When did you ask God to make you a bold preacher? When did you ask for "all the boldness needed to speak?" Are you afraid to ask; do you fear the consequences of asking? After all, God might hear and answer your prayer! Then where would you be? Right, getting yourself into a lot of trouble, like Paul and Peter and Stephen! That would never do, would it? But, notice the interesting dilemma that I have just sketched: you are afraid to pray for boldness because you might get it, and you fear what would happen as a consequence. But don't you see the fallacy in that sort of reasoning? You would not fear any longer if you did

---

2. Lest any hypersensitive brothers be offended by Paul's bold words, let me observe that these words are immediately preceded by this comment: "But Saul (who is called Paul), filled with the Holy Spirit, looked straight at him and said. . . ."

become bold; as a matter of fact, you fear such consequences only because you *now* fear consequences. It will all change when the Lord answers your prayer.

Will God answer? Yes. As his record clearly shows, Peter was not always bold. Like a good father, God will not give you a snake or a scorpion if you ask for a fish or an egg. He even reasons with you about the matter: "So, then, if you who are evil know how to give good gifts to your children, how much more will the heavenly Father give the Holy Spirit to those who ask Him?" (Luke 11: 11-13). The Spirit produces holy boldness; will you ask Him for it?

This boldness will not come in the form of a surge of feeling by which you will immediately recognize that it has been given to you. But, as you step forward in faith and obedience, again and again to speak with frankness and honesty, with directness and clarity, you will discover that the fear of man will have less and less influence on what you say. Pray, speak, and learn.

6
Preaching from God's Heart

We have been thinking not only about what it means to preach to the heart, but also about how it is done. So far, we have discovered that the preacher himself must cultivate the right kind of heart so that he may preach in the power of the Holy Spirit with boldness. But what does he preach?

He preaches a message that comes from God's heart. This terminology, "God's heart," at first may trouble you as it did me. But then I discovered this year that in the Bible God Himself does not hesitate to speak of His heart. For instance, He calls David, "a man after My own heart" (I Sam. 13:14), meaning one who is in sympathy with His own thoughts and concerns. In Jeremiah, the notion of God's heart appears again and again: 3:15; 7:31; 19:5; 23:20; 30:24; 32:35,41, often in speaking of some idea never having come into God's heart[1] (there, the meaning of heart as "thoughts" or "mind" is very clear). But, especially, Jeremiah speaks of the time when God says that He will provide "shepherds according to My heart, who will feed you knowledge and understanding" (Jer. 3:15). This passage is important to us.

The preachers God uses are men who are *after* (literally, "as") His heart. That is to say, they understand God's purposes and His ways, they are in harmony with them, and they are anxious to tell others about them. The concerns they have were first God's concerns. Such shepherds feed God's flock what He wants them to: "knowledge and understanding." Where do they get it? From His Word. Men who preach to the heart, then, are men who know God's Word, who personally accept and are molded by God's Word, and who, as a result, are capable of feeding others on that life-giving and nourishing Word. So, the preacher must

1. This, of course, is anthropomorphic language.

be capable of understanding God's Word and feeding others on it.

A preacher who is filled with the Spirit is also filled with the Spirit's message. He does not preach what he wants to preach; he preaches what the Spirit has caused to be written. In a peculiar sense, the Bible is the Spirit's Book. He carried its writers along, enabling them to write it error-free (II Pet. 1:21); when Scripture is quoted, often we are told, as we are in Hebrews 3:7, "The Spirit says. . . ."

Prophets sent from God frequently began their writings with words something like these: "The burden of the Word of the Lord to Israel by Malachi" (Mal. 1:1). What do those words mean? The Hebrew word translated "burden" means "something that is carried; a load." But because the Word of God was such a weighty thing for a man to carry to his fellow countrymen, this term was used of the prophetic message and, in time, came to mean "an oracle [especially a threatening one] from God."

The term never lost its idea of a burden or load to be borne. And it is exactly that fact that we must understand if we are to come to a full appreciation of what it means to preach to the heart. Sometimes we speak of "delivering" a message. That modern terminology fits quite well with the biblical notion of bearing a message. A preacher who thoroughly understands what he must say to his listeners, with all of its gravity and importance as the Word of God, goes into the pulpit weighed down with a burden. He has a burden on his heart. And it is not until he has accurately and faithfully conveyed that message to his listeners that he can truly be said to have "delivered" it. Because of the weight of responsibility involved in conveying God's Word to others, those who deliver it faithfully are also delivered of it. Only then is the weight of the responsibility lifted from their hearts. Men fail to preach to the heart when they do not feel that weight personally.

Paul experienced this weight. He tells us as much when he writes of himself as a "debtor" (Rom. 1:14) and when he cries out, "Woe to me if I don't announce the good news!" (I Cor. 9:16b). And something of that same necessity is discernible in the words of Peter and John: "We can't do anything but speak what we saw and heard" (Acts 4:20).

What is the message of the Lord that the preacher today must deliver? It consists of two elements: the gospel and the implications of the gospel in the lives of those who have believed it. The gospel is the news about the substitutionary, penal, sacrificial death of Christ for sinners and His bodily resurrection from the dead. The gospel's implications are all of those teachings Christ "commanded" His disciples to "observe" (Matt. 28:20). The preacher's twofold burden, therefore, is to proclaim a message of evangelism and sanctification.

The source of heart-reaching messages is the Bible. "Faith" comes from hearing the Word (Rom. 10:17). Prophets and apostles had direct revelation from God; today we have that same revelation in an inscripturated form. The idea of the written Word of God is not recent; it is biblical. The Bible calls itself God's Word (cf. esp. Ps. 119), despite what liberals confidently say to the contrary. So, if preachers wish not only to preach to the heart, but to preach in ways that are pleasing to God, they must preach "after [as] His heart." To do that, they must learn His thoughts and intents (heart) and become attuned to them in their own lives. They may learn from the Bible all that it is necessary to preach (cf. II Tim. 3:16, 17). Indeed, there is only one way to preach to hearts: to preach from God's heart; but God has revealed His heart only in His written Word.

I shall not discuss how best to interpret the Bible; I have said much about that in *What to Do on Thursday, Preaching with Purpose,* and *Truth Apparent,*[2] books in which I have stressed the need for *telic* preaching. The *telos* is the purpose of a preaching portion. Frequently preachers use the Scriptures for their own purposes rather than for the purposes for which the Holy Spirit gave them, thereby losing the power to preach to hearts. *Telic* preachers concentrate on discovering the Holy Spirit's purpose in any given passage and make that purpose their own. They make sure they use the preaching portion for the same purpose or purposes for which it was given. They struggle with a passage until they know what the Holy Spirit intended to do to the reader by means of that passage, and they make that also the intention of their sermon. That is the way to discover and preach the heart of God. Only the one who knows His heart can become a shepherd who is after God's heart, feeding His flock on His knowledge and under-

2. Published by Presbyterian and Reformed Publishing Co.

standing. Precisely how one discovers the *telos* of a passage, what implications that *telos* has on other aspects of preaching, etc., is discussed in the books that I have mentioned at the beginning of this paragraph.

As important as illustrations and examples may be to make a biblical truth clear, memorable, and personal, illustrations and examples may never replace God's Word in preaching. Preachers who choose a theme and string illustrations along it like beads err greatly; they must learn, rather, to preach from the thoughts and mind of God. Paul asks, "Who knows the thoughts of a person except the spirit of the person in him?" Then, he points out, "So too no one knows God's thoughts except God's Spirit" (I Cor. 2:11). And, in the Scriptures, he observes, "To us God revealed it by His Spirit. The Spirit searches into everything, even the deep thoughts of God" (v. 10). Because of the Spirit's revelation in the Scriptures, together with His illuminating power within the believer, Paul can declare, ". . . we have the mind of Christ" (v. 16).

How tragic, therefore, that men in the pulpit prattle on about the ideas of other men, share their own opinions, and feed God's sheep on diets of everything else. All the while, food provided by God—available, nourishing, life giving—is almost totally neglected. Preacher, you will preach to the heart only when you preach from God's heart. You will preach from God's heart only when you know what is in His heart. And you will know what is in His heart only when you know His Word. You must dedicate yourself, therefore, to a thorough study of that Word so that you will truly become a workman in the Word who does not need to be ashamed, because you have accurately handled the Word of truth (II Tim. 2:15) in your preaching.

7
Heart-Convicting Preaching

Not all preaching involves conviction of sin. There is preaching that is primarily informative, preaching that brings encouragement and assistance to the listener, and preaching that lifts one's heart in doxology to God.[1] But, in this chapter, we are concerned with the sort of preaching that leads to conviction of sin.

We have seen that preaching to the heart is preaching in which the Holy Spirit is intimately involved. Because that is so, we must consider the matter of conviction. Jesus told us that "when He [the Spirit] comes, He will convict the world about sin, about righteousness and about judgment" (John 16:8). Since we must preach the gospel to the world, and it is the mission of the Holy Spirit to convict the world, the heart-piercing message that Peter preached is a message that convicts. But, as we have seen, the other aspect of the church's preaching is to the church itself; does it also include a message that convicts? Yes. There are any number of passages to which one might refer, but I would turn your attention only to the following: "All Scripture is breathed out by God and useful for teaching, for conviction, for correction and for disciplined training in righteousness" (II Tim. 3:16). In preaching "the Word," Timothy is commanded, "Be at it in season and out of season. Convict, reprove, urge with complete patience and full teaching" (II Tim. 4:2).

We must examine the term that is translated "convict" and then look in some detail at the verses that have just been men-

---

1. But even in this sort of preaching, where the emphasis is on something else, the need for conviction is frequently present. How can one praise God, and at the same time not be reminded of his own unworthiness? The need for encouragement and assistance often points to one's failure to seek out the same sooner, or to his lack of diligence in doing so. New information leads to new responsibilities and the recognition of sin previously unknown.

tioned. But, before we do, let me point out once more, as Paul does in writing to Timothy, that listeners will be "convicted" when the Scriptures are preached. The God-breathed Scriptures are the means that the Spirit uses in convicting the listener because they are the source of His message. Preachers should not depend on harranging, the use of sob stories, and the like to bring about conviction; rather, they must depend upon a faithful proclamation of biblical truth to do the job. The Spirit uses His Word, as it is faithfully preached, to convict of sin.

Let us consider, then, the term that is translated "convict." Some versions read "rebuke" or "reprove" instead of "convict." These translations are too weak. The Holy Spirit does not merely make charges; He fully substantiates them. The term *elengcho* comes from the law courts. It means not only to prefer charges, but also to so pursue the case against the one who is charged that he is *convicted* of the crime of which he is accused. The one who convicts *proves another guilty*. The Holy Spirit is our lawyer (*parakletos* = lawyer). He defends us from Satan, the accuser of the brethren. He pleads the blood of Christ before the judgment throne of God. But He is not only our defense attorney, our counselor-at-law; He is also the prosecuting attorney, bringing the case against those who must be convicted. So, the term means, then, to prove a charge.

That is what Jesus had in mind when He said that the Holy Spirit would "convict the world about sin, about righteousness and about judgment" (John 16:8). The Holy Spirit has come to make His case, and when He finishes doing so, men stand exposed for what they are. He cuts through all of the fog and confusion and brings conviction by His Word that what He has charged is correct.

Now, Jesus explains the Spirit's case against the world. He takes each of the three elements in the case and extrapolates on it. He says:

> . . . about sin—because they don't believe in Me, about righteousness—because I am going to My Father and you won't see Me any more, and about judgment—because this world's ruler has been judged (John 16:9-11).

Just what does He mean by these explanations?

The Spirit will convict the world (in John's writings, *world* frequently is used to refer to Gentiles as well as Jews, in contrast to Jews only). His activities will be worldwide in scope. Commenting on this passage, Calvin asks, "For how comes it that the voice proceeding from the mouth of a man [in preaching] penetrates into hearts, takes root there, and at length yields fruit, changing hearts of stone into hearts of flesh, and renewing men, but because the Spirit of Christ quickens it?" As Hendriksen puts it, He came to "publicly *expose its guilt and call it to repentance.*"

His case against the world involves three things: sin, righteousness, and judgment. He proves His case by affirming the sin of the world, which is clearly evidenced in its unbelief, by demonstrating the righteousness of Christ, which is plainly proved in His resurrection and ascension, and by declaring the dethronement of the Devil, which is unmistakably implied in his judgment on the cross. This case is foolproof; the world has no answer to it. It constitutes the biblical message of the gospel: Christ came to die for sinners, rose from the dead, and defeated the evil one.

But the Spirit also convicts the church of sin. Sanctification is a process that often involves such conviction. That process is set forth in II Timothy 3:16. There, four elements stand out: the Scriptures are useful for (1) teaching, (2) *conviction,* (3) correction, and (4) disciplined training in righteousness. That is to say, the preacher uses the Bible (v. 17) to teach God's standards, to show us how we have failed to measure up to them, to tell us how to get ourselves out of the messes we get ourselves into because of our sins, and to help us to avoid falling into the same sins again in the future. Conviction comes from teaching God's truth about His requirements for believers and about how our failure to live according to them displeases the Savior who died for them.

When Paul wrote, "Preach the Word. . . . Convict, reprove, urge with complete patience and full teaching," he was saying practically the same thing. Surely, in some pulpits today, there is far too little preaching that convicts and rebukes. In others, there is rebuking enough, but there is little or no patience with people, and often very little teaching about precisely what changes God requires and how to make them. It is very likely that the verb translated "urge" might better be translated "assist" (*parakaleo* has that more general meaning in most passages and refers to doing or saying whatever is necessary to help another accomplish something). Certainly, if it is a fault of some preachers not to rebuke, it is a fault of many others who, having rebuked, fail to help their listeners make the necessary changes. (For more on implementation of one's teaching see *What to Do on Thursday* and *Preaching with Purpose*.)

So, both unbelievers and believers need to experience the penetrating power of the Word as it cuts through to the heart. The writer of Hebrews spoke of this power of the Word. Here is what he said:

> God's Word is alive and active, sharper than any two-edged sword, penetrating deeply enough to cut open soul and spirit and joints and marrow; it can judge the desires and thoughts of the heart. And before Him no creature can hide, but all are naked and vulnerable to the eyes of Him to Whom we must give an account (Heb. 4:12, 13).

There is a description, under the figure of a sword, of the Bible's power to penetrate to the deepest recesses of the heart. There is nothing in a man's life that the Scriptures cannot touch, no area that can escape their probing thrust. The Scriptures are entirely adequate to convict of any and every sin. The Bible strips us of all our defenses and cuts us open before God's eyes like fallen warriors, totally vulnerable. It lays open the soul and the spirit (not divides between them, as some wrongly interpret); it discloses both the thoughts and the desires of the heart. No man can stand before it, claiming his innocence. It convicts; the Spirit uses His written Word as it is preached to pierce through to men's hearts.

But, there will be no conviction of sin unless the Word is used, and used properly. That means that it will be used boldly, appropriately, and fully as Paul used it when he reminded the Ephesian elders,

> I didn't hold back in declaring anything that was beneficial to you. . . . ; I haven't held back in declaring God's whole counsel to you" (Acts 20:20, 27).

There is often a tendency for a preacher to "hold back" precisely what may benefit the congregation, for fear that he may get himself in trouble. The result is that the whole counsel of God is not proclaimed. Hard truths are either bypassed or soft-pedaled. Unpopular doctrines, if preached at all, are served in such small quantities or in such a diluted form that they could hardly be described as that sort of "healthy [i.e., health-promoting] teaching" that Paul required of preachers when writing to Timothy. But the tendency of preachers to hold back is dangerous. Paul said, "So then, I testify to you this day that I am clean from everybody's blood because I haven't held back . . ." (Acts 20:26, 27[a]). Clearly, those who hold back are not. No wonder James warned, "My brothers, not many of you should be teachers, because you know that we teachers will receive stricter judgment" (James 3:1).

Preacher, do you preach the Word in order to gain conviction? Do you preach the Word with all of its inherent force and power? Do you preach all of the Word, or only those portions that you think will be readily acceptable to your hearers? Is anyone's blood on your head?

8
A Heart-Adapted Form

We have seen how necessary it is to preach boldly the whole counsel of God in the power of the Spirit in order to bring conviction. But, at the close of the last chapter, I began to mention another matter—form. There are a number of ways in which those who do care to proclaim God's truth boldly nevertheless do fail—largely because of poor form. In this chapter, we shall take up this matter in some depth.

In Colossians 4:3, 4, Paul wrote:

> . . . praying at the same time also about us, that God may open for us a door for the Word, to speak about the secret of Christ, because of which I am in bonds, so that I may proclaim it clearly, as I ought to.

To "proclaim it clearly, as I ought to"—those words have to do with form.

Sometimes, those who would be "more pious than Paul" try to tell us that form is unimportant. So long as the truth is proclaimed, what more is there to do? It is God's Word, they say, not our eloquence, that gets the job done. There are both truth and error in those statements.

Of course it is not our eloquence that changes people. Paul made that point in I Corinthians 2:1-5. But here, in Colossians, Paul is so deeply concerned about clarity (a matter of form) that he urges the Colossian church to pray about the matter. Does Paul contradict himself—in one place denouncing those who focus on form and, in another, stressing its importance? No, there is no contradiction. Eloquence was not Paul's concern. He told the Corinthians that he wanted their faith to rest only on the power of the Spirit; he did not want them drawn into some false profession of faith based on the clever rhetoric of men. Studied eloquence, rhetorical gimmicks, and the like are to be scrapped. But that does not mean all concern about form must be avoided. Paul was not interested in becoming a Demosthenes, but his aim was to preach in a *form that is appropriate to the message*. Notice, his concern is for clarity. That, as I said, is a matter of form. And his comment is that the preacher is obligated to be clear ("as I *ought to*" speak). The desire to be clear and the desire to be eloquent are two entirely different things.

Paul's one goal was to avoid anything that might obscure God's truth and to do everything that he could to present it as clearly as possible. There is no contradiction between that desire and an unwillingness to have his listeners' faith depend upon something other than the gospel of Christ. In fact, the two concerns dovetail: if anything obscures the gospel, it isn't possible for people to understand and believe it. Preacher, that means that you must not seek to become a Demosthenes, calling attention to your rhetorical powers, but you must do whatever is necessary to be sure that your proclamation of the convicting, nourishing Word is clear. You must aim not at the applause of men, but at reaching their hearts.

Clarity is the one prerequisite pertaining to form that is essential to preaching to the heart. How sad it is that preachers do not work more on this matter of clarity. How important it must be if the apostle Paul himself was concerned enough about it to ask for prayer. Have you ever asked your congregation to pray for clarity in your preaching? Have you ever asked them to pray about your preaching at all?

Terminology can obscure. The great theological words of the Bible cannot be abandoned, but neither should they be preached without clear definition. I do not mean that you must always say, in so many words, "Justification is. . . ." No, often, having used the word, you may include a definition in the same sentence: "If you believe, God will justify you, declaring you righteous and counting you perfect in His sight."

There are, however, many terms that might be reserved for teaching in more explicitly doctrinal settings. Words like eschatology and soteriology do not need to be used in the pulpit. Yet, some men, perhaps thinking that they will be viewed as erudite, constantly use language that hinders rather than facilitates the presentation of the message. Others, whose hearts may be right, simply carry the language of the seminaries and the commentaries over into the pulpit. This too is a mistake.

Sometimes the cultivation of a "preaching style" with its quasi-Elizabethan language obscures. A wall plaque reads, "ESCHEW OBFUSCATION." It might be well to print up your own copy and keep it under the glass on the desk in the study. Obviously, the word "obfuscation" raises a flag against all stilted, technical, or otherwise unclear modern terminology, while the word "eschew" pokes fun at outdated and archaic terms. This "preaching style" seems to relish such vocabulary. You may find that you will have to spend time studying your own usage in order to discover whether you are guilty of obscuring the truth when you preach. The New Testament was largely written by simple men using the street language of the day. Paul, a highly educated man, found it necessary to work at not allowing his educational habits to get in the way of clarity in preaching. You will have to do the same.

Of course, there are many preachers whose grammar is incorrect and whose syntax is sloppy. They have never learned how to speak plainly and accurately. While stressing clarity, the Bible puts no premium on sloppiness. Indeed, sloppy grammar and syntax themselves tend to obscure. People find themselves saying, "Did he mean this . . . or that?" Clarity is a matter of simplicity rather than ornateness; it consists of plainness of speech rather than eloquence or eruditeness; and it focuses on accuracy of grammar and syntax rather than sloppiness.

How effective is your preaching style? If it is defective in one or more of these ways, your style may get in the way of the message and keep it from penetrating your listener's heart. It will matter little how much preparation you may have done to obtain the finest food to feed the flock; it will not make much difference whether you present your message boldly or not; if what you have to say is unclear, everything you do may be in vain. Clarity is the thing. Paul was right—that is how he was to speak; preacher, it is also how you ought to speak.

9
Conclusion

You have been faced with a challenge. In this short book I have not attempted to treat every aspect of the subject, but only those which might, in a practical way, challenge you to thought and deeper commitment. You know better than anyone else what deficiencies there are in your preaching. It is my prayer that this book will not only stir you again to the hope of preaching to hearts with power, but also to act on that hope.

Now that you know what is required, what will you do about it? Filled with good intentions, will you put down the book and allow yourself to be caught up in the many other affairs that make demands on you, never to go beyond hopes and good resolutions? That is what your congregation so often does after you have preached effectively and reached their hearts. Will you follow their lead, or will you be a leader who, himself, is able to demonstrate that he is capable of doing differently?

If the words of this book have reached your heart, admit it to yourself. Tell God about it, and then lay out a plan for doing what must be done to effect the needed changes. It is my observation that unless busy people determine exactly what must be done and then set out a schedule for doing it, little will be accomplished. Making the changes that are necessary for preaching to the heart will take some time and effort—especially regular, disciplined effort. Changes will not be made, therefore, unless there is a commitment to make them, coupled with a plan for bringing them about. Are you willing to listen to the conviction of your heart?

If so, let me suggest that you use the blank space that follows to lay out that plan. You will want more specific help such as that which is found in *Preaching with Purpose,* an earlier textbook on preaching, written with the intention of giving just such help to those who need it. Put down all that you need to do, and *date each element in your plan*. May the God of all grace give you great grace as He enables you to work at becoming a preacher of the Word to the hearts of men!

PLAN